W9-AKD-496

Life Undercover

Life Undercover

*COMING OF AGE
IN THE CIA*

Amaryllis Fox

RANDOM HOUSE
LARGE PRINT

Cover image courtesy of Amaryllis Fox
Cover design by Jenny Carrow

The Library of Congress has established a
Cataloging-in-Publication record for this title.

ISBN: 978-0-593-16821-9

www.penguinrandomhouse.com/large-print-format-books

FIRST LARGE PRINT EDITION

Printed in the United States of America

10 9 8 7 6 5 4 3 2 1

This Large Print edition published in accord
with the standards of the N.A.V.H.

For my mum, who taught me
to live without cover

Life Undercover

1

In the glass, I can see the man who's trailing me. I first noticed him a few turns back, his path correlated with mine in the mess of Karachi back alleys. Our reflections mingle in the tailor's window. He is horse-faced and tall. His palms open and close as he walks. "The security of the veil," a poster reads, above burqas and hijabs.

Ahead of me, the bus I'd planned to board comes and goes, covered in an ecstasy of pigment and pattern. Every square inch is painted with bright shapes and swirls, intricate and infinite, like a Mardi Gras parade float, a diesel temple to the pleasure of the eye. It has the look of a free thing burdened, a slow-lumbering dragon, weighed down by its own beauty and the commuters that hang from its belly and back. They are my favorite thing about Pakistan, these buses. Against the dust and the smog and the honking of horns, they are startling, like the discovery of a kindred soul behind the otherwise dull face of a stranger.

It won't delay me long, letting this one lumber by. Another will come through in a few minutes on its way to M. A. Jinnah Road. Better not to give Mr. Ed the impression that I'm trying to lose him. Nothing raises suspicions more than shaking surveillance. It's what always makes me laugh about the CIA operatives in the movies. All the roof gymnastics and juggling of Glocks. In real life, one chase sequence through a city center and my cover would be blown for life. Better to lull them into a false sense of security. Walk slowly enough for them to keep up. Stop at yellow lights when driving. Give them a good look each time I come and go. In other words, bore them to tears. Then slip out and save the Bond business for when they've been left to tranquil sleep.

I can see Mr. Ed fiddling with cooking utensils at a market stall while we wait. It's not clear which flavor of surveillant he is. First guess is usually the local service—a counter-intelligence officer from the government of whatever country I'm in. But in this case, I'm not so sure. Pakistani intelligence operatives are good at what they do. Their surveillance teams are usually six or seven strong, so that they can swap out the guy who's trailing me every few turns to minimize the chance that I'll notice. This man seems to be alone. Not only that, but there's a foreign angle to his face. Despite his traditional dress, the kameez worn long and loose over his trousers, he has the air of central Asia about him. A Kazakh, maybe, or an Uzbek. Most likely, he's checking me out in preparation for tomorrow's meeting. Al Qa'ida has had an influx of central Asian recruits of late. Putting newcomers to work as spotters is pretty typical. Gives them a chance to learn the city while the group's recruiters size them up.

I watch him weave his way through the stalls that line the side of Jodia Bazar. He picks up part of a carburetor and turns it around in his hands. Something about the way he examines it makes me wonder whether maybe he's of the third variety—an aspiring arms broker who knows I work with Jakab, the Hungarian purveyor of all things Soviet surplus. Of course, there's always the underwhelming fourth possibility: he's a plain old would-be predator, eyeing a twenty-eight-year-old American girl traipsing through foreign streets alone. After all, there's Occam's razor to consider. The simplest explanation is usually the right one.

Government or goon, any tail is cause to abort an operation. No sense meeting a source or picking up dropped documents with an audience in tow. Even harmless creeps can turn less harmless when they think they've witnessed something worth telling. Luckily, I'm not on my way to an operational act. Not until tomorrow. Today is pure reconnaissance.

Jakab told me the intersection of Abdullah Haroon and Sarwar Shaheed. That was all he knew, he said. He wasn't even supposed to know that. He'd probed his buyers for the info, under the guise of selling them the right bomb for the job. He'd need to understand the target, he told them, to be sure the material would be enough to register on a Geiger counter. Enough to win them the attention they sought.

When the next bus arrives, I board slowly and easily, as if I'm not headed to check out the target of a potential nuclear terror attack. Mr. Ed climbs up top, to sit on the roof. I take a seat in the women's compartment. Outside, the afternoon is fading into gloaming and the motorbikes begin to turn on their lights. There's time, amid the crush of evening traffic, to take in the buildings, most of them older than the country itself, monuments to a time when Pakistan and India were one, the plaything of colonists and kings. I feel the kinship of it, being a Yankee. The shrugging off of England's yoke. I can picture the men and women around me tossing crates of tea into the ocean in their kameezes and shawls. We are rebel lands, they and us. If only all that rebellion didn't spill quite so much blood.

I can see the intersection emerge from the traffic and the donkey carts, up beyond the faded tarps, strung taut between buildings to lend shelter from the now-set sun. On one side is the National Bank of Pakistan, a reasonable guess at their objective, I suppose. After all, the mullahs cleared the twin towers as legitimate military targets, claiming that America kills Muslims as much by impoverishing the innocent as it does by tank treads on the ground. But the building doesn't feel right to me. It's concrete and uninspiring, postwar brutalism at its most scathingly bare. It doesn't exactly scream Western excess.

I wait until the driver slows and jump back into the dust of the city. Mr. Ed lands softly on the far side of the bus. I cross Abdullah Haroon Road slowly enough for him to follow, and then it dawns on me as I reach the other side. In front of me, set back slightly behind chained gates, is what looks to be a miniature castle, a tiny stone fortress amid the rickshaws and pigeons. It's the Karachi Press Club, the bastion of free speech and independent journalism, famed home to protest, debate, and the only bar serving alcohol in the country. Dollars to doughnuts, this is their target. Nothing like getting bombed to get you bombed in this town.

From what Jakab said, this attack would be intended as a warning—a shot across the bow of any country where the press flows as free as the booze. Clean up Pakistan first, then turn attention to the infidel. It's an elegant positioning, but the truth is that it's a lot easier to plan and execute an attack here than in Times Square. Al Qa'ida's been working toward a nuclear capability since at least 1992, when Usama bin Laden sent his first envoys to Chechnya in search of fissile material lost in the crumbling Soviet shuffle. But washed-up nukes are elusive, expensive, and highly temperamental. Makes sense they'd aim for a dry run close to home.

That means I'm looking at two scenes simultaneously: first, the potential attack in front of me and, second, the implications for a follow-up attack on U.S. soil. Writers and thinkers from across the world come to speak at the Karachi Press Club, including Americans. A ten-kiloton nuclear weapon would vaporize every building and every person I can see for half a mile. Detonated outside the **New York Times** building in midtown Manhattan, the same device would incinerate Times Square, Penn Station, Bryant Park, and the New York Public Library, plus countless apartments, bodegas, preschools, and taxicabs in a blast burning hotter than the sun. Because light travels faster than sound, the half million or so people in that first radius would turn to vapor before they even heard a boom. For another half mile in every direction, radiation would kill most people within days. Cancer would ravage their outer neighbors for years yet to come.

Terrorism is a psychological game of escalation. It's not the last attack that scares people. It's the next one.

Think it's frightening to see our embassies hit overseas, as they were in Kenya and Tanzania in 1998? Try watching a fortified battleship blown up on active duty, as our USS **Cole** was in the Gulf of Aden two years later. Think a strike on our military is scary? How about a mass-casualty attack on our homeland, like the one we watched unfold in horror on a cloudless Tuesday morning the following September.

The question for al Qa'ida since 9/11 has been where to go from there. What could offer more haunting imagery than jetliners plowing into skyscrapers? What could be more destructive than killing three thousand people on a random Tuesday morning? Eventually the only thing left is a mushroom-shaped cloud. Eventually the only viable escalation is a blast so bright, the few surviving witnesses will see its image burned on their retinas for the remainder of their lives.

Mr. Ed is watching a woman walk through the Karachi Press Club gates. Her head is covered with a 1970s Pucci-style scarf. The bottom of her kameez is patched with flowers. The whole look is demure and Islamic with a joyful Partridge Family wink. Beside the gates, a man sells flowers, cut and bunched. He shouts discounted prices at drivers' windows. On the sidewalk behind him, there's a sign for a children's dentist.

I feel the horror of it froth inside me. The evisceration. The hideous, useless waste of potential. I want to run at the horse-faced man, want to rush him and shake him and ask him how he can consider killing a woman who sews flowers onto her clothes. How he can consider killing half a million like her. But for all I know, he's a run-of-the-mill street stalker. I'll have my chance tomorrow. One shot to tell al Qa'ida why they shouldn't detonate a nuclear weapon in a major city center. One opportunity, face-to-face with the group that wants to bring this country to its knees.

Leave the man alone, I figure.

Then he takes out a mobile phone and makes eye contact with me as he dials.

2

My dad is like a spreadsheet: logical, data-driven, and capable of crunching as many inputs as he's given. He's American, raised in Franklinville, New York, a town so small and insular, he was among only a few kids in his graduating class to go to college. He went to the University of Chicago and became one of the youngest economics professors in its history. By the time my older brother, Ben, and I come along, he's advising foreign governments on energy policy in every corner of the globe, which means we see him mainly on his way to and from the airport.

In those early days, my mom's more like an Impressionist painting: beautiful, proper, and destined to someday—though then not yet—slip the rules of form and burst into her own abstract truth. She is the color in our coloring book, the aliveness in our mornings, noons, and nights. She's English. And like all Brits, she grew up marinated in tradition and protocol. In my earliest memories, she's still bound by the rules of class that permeate the social circles of English country manors. A wild poet in her youth, her mother reined in her fierce brilliance, taught her the importance of the right habits, the right language, the right education, to flourish in the strange waters of British aristocracy. And in my earliest memories, she still wonders whether to pass those rules along. A gift of love for we children who are her everything. But an artist still at heart, she opts instead to let us be blank canvases, and slowly, bravely, comes to let our color live outside the lines.

My brother has learning differences. Sometimes they mean he doesn't sense the lines at all. Wildly clever, but challenged in motor skills and speech, he's mercilessly teased by the banal bullies of our school in Washington, D.C. My mom is determined to mend Ben's differences for fear others might be cruel, might categorize him as the wrong sort or think of him as different.

Like a Sherpa, determined to get her charge over Everest's peak, Mom sits patiently with Ben at our little kitchen table, math book open to a sea of numbers he complains won't sit still on the page. They move about like pixies, he says, and I watch from the cupboard under the sink, in case one flies up in the air where I can see it. I've converted the cupboard into a playhouse, with pictures of clouds on the wall made from dried Elmer's glue. Every so often, my brother gives up feigning understanding when he knows there is none and turns to my hideaway in exhausted despair. I hold up our old terrier Snowy's paw in a solidarity salute or make our pet hermit crabs chant his name in the air until finally he cracks a big toothy grin and my mother laughs her beautiful laugh and they stop to make popcorn—the kind with the built-in frying pan that swells like a pregnant belly on top of the stove.

On the weekends, Ben and I roam happily around the Smithsonian, just the two of us. Mom drops us off across from Uncle Beazley, the hollow fiberglass triceratops, with horns polished pale by a thousand climbing hands. She synchronizes our watches, gives us solemn instructions about cars and strangers (even if they say they have puppies), and calls out how much she loves us as we bound up the stairs.

We watch the Gilgamesh movie in the Mesopotamia room of the natural history museum. It's stop-motion animation, with clay characters that jolt as they walk. At the Air and Space, we eat dehydrated ice cream and watch the Man in the Moon talk about history and war and the changes he's witnessed from his spot in the sky, which, my brother points out, makes the Gilgamesh story seem like one little stripe in a big Neapolitan sundae.

When the weather's nice, we hang around at the Lincoln Memorial and take turns reciting the Gettysburg Address, wearing traffic cones as top hats. Then five minutes before our synchronized minute hands approach five p.m., we race back to the infinity sculpture and our mom's waiting car. The underground parking lot's been closed. To make it harder to plant a bomb, Mom explains.

I start school and learn that Ben differs from other kids in ways I think make him cool and they think make him prey. He walks with a quirky stiffness. "Like a freak," the bullies sneer. "Like Gilgamesh," I tell him. On the playground, he spends recess sitting in the shade of a tree, humming strange pieces of music with long gaps of silence in them. The other kids think he has a screw loose, but I know he's just working his way through whichever symphony my dad's played on our record player the night before. Humming each instrument's part from beginning to end. Violin, then clarinet, then kettledrums. He takes music apart the way a tinkerer deconstructs a radio. Can hear how it all fits together in his head.

"Every village needs an idiot," the bullies laugh.

Every genius is misunderstood.

In the evenings, Mom reads to us. Paddington and **The Lion, the Witch, and the Wardrobe** and **The Wolves of Willoughby Chase.** She does all the voices, stopping only when she's made us laugh or cry so hard she can't help joining in. Then we all collect ourselves and dive back into the pages, which dance and flicker around us, until finally our pleas for one more chapter run out and we drift to sleep in lands far away from math books and schoolyard bullies. "Never forget," she tells us softly, "you can travel anywhere, just by closing your eyes."

When I am seven and Ben is ten, we save up cereal box tops to send away for a cardboard haunted house. It comes in a flat pack and we set it up in our basement, slotting the pieces together until we have our own spooky castle, between the washing machine and the stairs.

The light's pretty dim down there, filtered through dusty subterranean windows, so we use my plastic glowworm as a lantern, which means leaving him in the sunlit garden every second day to charge. From time to time, Mom comes down to do the washing, but other than that, our kingdom is pretty impervious to the world beyond.

I wear roller skates and my brother builds houses out of Lincoln Logs, dwarfed by our giant cardboard spookhouse. "We have to protect the villagers," he says. We stage action figures around the cabins and keep Ben's plastic vampire bat inside the haunted castle, in case maybe it scares them. "Snowy will defend them," I croon, brushing the old dog's wiry fur as he sleeps on the floor. Sometimes Ben's old teddy bear Chester comes down to sit beside him, lumpy and lopsided.

We're down in that basement one day, fending off spaceship attacks, when my mother pads down the stairs to tell us that Ben's letter has come. It's his acceptance to Wicken Park, the English boarding school he's supposed to attend before Eton.

"What if he doesn't like it?" I ask. "What if they're mean to him?" My mother sits down on the bottom step.

"Well, then he can write to tell us," she says

gently. "And we'll take him away." She turns to Ben. "The teachers will probably read your letters, though, so we'll need a code word. One that wouldn't be used in normal letter writing, so you don't use it by mistake."

It's confusing, why we're sending Ben somewhere he might need a code word to escape. I don't even know what Wicken Park looks like, can't picture the place that's stealing my brother in my mind. I glance at the cartoon monsters on the side of the spookhouse. One of them has a jagged blank face where the tape's pulled off the ink. It's the most frightening.

"What about 'haunted house'?" I ask.

"Perfect," Mom says and gives us both a tight squeeze.

———

We treat every day of the hot, sticky summer that follows like numbered jewels, noting every time an activity might be our last—the last time we pick mulberry leaves for Ben's silkworms in our quest to produce a parachute; the last time we walk the wooden locks across the Georgetown canals, playing brave sailors atop the evil pirates' plank; the last time we sit in the way back of our parents' station wagon on our way to the John Brown Wax Museum, with its muskets and its freedom fighters and its hooded hangman's rope.

In the midst of those last months, my mother's belly begins to swell like the popcorn frying pan on the stove and our parents tell us we're going to have a sister.

The news doesn't really register until we both come down with chicken pox and Mom has to move to a hotel to protect the growing baby. We howl for her, demanding that she read us stories over the phone, then declaring crossly that it isn't the same. Our dad does his best to distract us. He plays Carl Sagan lectures on the record player. We join in when Carl says "billions" in his magic, echoey voice. But it's not as much fun the third or fourth time, so he switches it to Billy Crystal and we all shout, "You look marvelous!" even though we're covered with welts.

When the records run out, Dad breaks out the big guns. He teaches us to make a Mobius strip. Loop a strip of paper into a circle, add a twist in the middle, tape the ends together, and "ta-da," he says, "you've made eternity." I look at him like he's crazy, but then he tells me to draw a line along the surface without taking my pen off the paper and it ends up going all the way around, one long, continuous streak that marks both sides, like magic.

"I think it's probably worth getting chicken pox to learn how to make eternity," Ben says to me. "Don't you think?" Then my grandmother arrives to help, and our delicious, stolen sliver of Dad's attention slips away, like sunlight under a closed cupboard door.

That Fourth of July, Ben and I stand on the crumbling brick wall overlooking the Potomac docks as the fireworks crash-boom through the sky. "Imagine that's the sound of the British approaching," Ben says. I close my eyes and imagine hard. An army is coming to kill our family. With every crash, they get closer. I start to cry. And for the first time, I understand that fireworks aren't always for fun.

The next week, Antonia is born. She's only a baby, though, and doesn't make up for the fact that Ben is going to be gone. Mom takes to sleeping under her crib because she cries so much in the night. Then, at summer's end, she comes with us, in her soft, pink clothes, to deliver Ben to school across the sea.

We drive through the deep of the English countryside to Wicken Park, an imposing stone manor house straight out of a Dickensian movie set. Ben and I stand side by side in the

circular drive, watching the other boys arrive
with their big trunks and foppish hair. The
palm of Ben's hand is pressed into mine, and
I can feel it shaking. The school looks like
our cardboard spookhouse. **Well, we picked
the right code word,** I think. But I don't say
that out loud. Instead, I go for "Pretty good
kingdom to protect from the pirates!" and he
nods with so much courage, it's hard for me
to swallow. Finally, the tears spill out of him.

"Crying like a little girl," one of the foppish
boys crows. "Boo-hoo. Better stay home and
play with your sister." I drop Ben's hand to
protect him from their teasing. Then suddenly
he is gone, swept up by the brusque matron
and hustled through the doors. I can still feel
the warmth of his fear in my palm.

We stand for a while, looking at the windows, in case he should find one and wave,
but their panes just reflect the chill of the
evening sky.

—

Almost as soon as we get home, the furniture
in our house begins to find its way into packing boxes. My dad tells me we're moving to
England, too. Not to the countryside, like

Ben, but to London, where he's going to advise Maggie Thatcher's government on what to do with the coal industry. I watch through the window as my parents hand Snowy to a couple who pulls up in a VW van. I go downstairs and sit in the spookhouse alone.

When we arrive in London, I claim the top-floor bedroom. It has a sloped ceiling, tucked under the eaves, and a window I take to climbing through, once my mom's read me a story, kissed my hair, and turned out the lights. I sit there most nights, balanced on the roof shingles, my feet tucked under my nightgown, watching Big Ben strike ten. The clock's a few blocks away, its giant face hanging in the night like a lost moon among the chimneys. And floating up there with it, I feel both small and vast.

Every month, Ben comes to London for the weekend to see us and we pad around Westminster Abbey and the Houses of Parliament, doing brass rubbings and making up stories about the poets and kings whose graves line the walls like chilly apartments. When we get home, baby Antonia is usually asleep and Mom has left a sign on the door, pleading with us to be as quiet as mice. We never tire of bursting inside, squeaking our loudest rodent impressions and collapsing into gales of laughter.

At the end of each visit, Ben gives me a hug and lets me believe he doesn't mind going back. I catch glimpses of the sorrow he's hiding. Little exchanges that end with a look asking me not to push further.

"How's Chester?"

"He's not around anymore."

"What happened to your head?"

"Fell."

"Who's your best friend?"

"Matron, I guess."

I wish he'd use the code word. Then Mom would pull him out and he'd be home and everything would go back to how it was. But he doesn't. He just gets quieter and taller, and soon even when he's home, he feels far away.

I start at the American School in St. John's Wood. There are cool kids there. I'm not one of them. I take refuge in two other outcasts, Lisa and Laura. When the cool girls start a club called the Pink Ladies and won't let us join, we start our own club, the Cool Cucumbers, and spend recess sweeping the playground to help out the custodian. When it rains, we build robots from discarded cardboard boxes. Peter the Postman is our masterpiece. A mailman robot, as tall as we are, with a locked box in his belly in which to leave secret notes.

Lisa and I get invited to a Pink Ladies sleepover. A girl named Cassie's birthday.

Feeling well out of our depth, we try to act grown-up, then promptly fall asleep. We're awoken in the middle of the night and put on trial for disturbing Cassie's mom. Cassie sits on a pile of pillows to act as the judge, and when the kangaroo court is finished, she sentences us to a night in her bedroom closet. We get locked in there together, amid Cassie's shoes and sparkly sequined dresses, until our mothers come to liberate us in the morning.

Somehow, the camaraderie outweighs the injury and we only grow closer. Laura and I write a dictionary for our own language and mock the cool kids in our new foreign tongue. Lisa shows me how to make a spiderweb of string all over my bedroom and hang bells on it to detect ghosts while we sleep. For three months, we are happy. Then the day after Christmas, my mother sits me down to tell me that Laura is dead. She was killed while flying home with her entire family, grandmother to infant brother, on the Pan Am flight bombed by Libyan terrorists over Lockerbie, Scotland. I am eight.

I fall quiet for long periods. I feel like my head is full of cotton. Feel sleepy and mute and numb. Finally, my dad teaches me to read the London **Times**. "You have to understand the forces that took her. It will seem less scary if you do." I think of the faceless monster on the cardboard spookhouse and I know that he is right.

Slowly my world is filled with a new cast of characters. Qaddafi and Thatcher and Reagan and Gorbachev. They sound like exotic fairy-tale people, wizards and witches and woodsmen living in distant magical forests. But their storybook showdowns can spill over into the real world, into my world, and steal my friends from the sky. So I have to pay attention.

By June, I'm transfixed by images of a solitary student, standing his ground in front of a line of Chinese tanks in a place called Tiananmen Square. **Tiananmen,** the articles note, means Gate of Heavenly Peace. I stare at the pictures for a long time. He does look peaceful. Peaceful and powerful, making all those soldiers stand down.

Other people see the man's power, too. By November, they're doing the same thing in Berlin, only this time they're knocking down a wall. The newspaper says that more than a hundred people have been killed trying to get to the other side of that wall. The first was a woman named Ida, who tried to jump from her apartment window to get to her sister's house. They'd always lived across from each other. Then overnight, the wall had appeared in the street between them and they hadn't been allowed to pass. It reminds me of the wall that's appeared between me and Laura. I root for the protesters as they hack it to pieces from on top of their cars.

3

We spend the summers at my mother's parents' house in the English countryside—a rambling old mansion with no proper heating, and mice in the cupboards. My grandfather is a British Raj sort of an antique who works in the city and is absent even when he's home. My grandmother is a onetime athlete, banished to a wheelchair by polio at thirty-five. She's funny and clever, so clever that she wrote all my grandfather's papers when they met at the University of Edinburgh, and it gets under her skin when his pretty, young secretaries eye her crumpled legs and reference her in the third person, like a patient with dementia.

"Does she need a blanket?" they ask, when they visit the house to take his dictation.

"No, she does not," my grandmother replies. "But she could use a gin and tonic."

My grandparents have adopted a son, Christian, from the Philippines, to keep them company now that their other children are grown. Christian and I are the same age, and my grandmother takes a sportswoman's delight in setting us against each other in all manner of competitions. Going to collect the mail becomes a grand running race the length of the tree-lined drive. Card games become tests of memory when we're challenged to recite the last twenty cards that were played, backward or by suit or rearranged into sequential order. Opening Christmas presents gets delayed until we've both swum the length of the pool under the ice that's formed on its surface, diving in one hole and emerging, panicked and breathless, from the other, my grandmother clicking a stopwatch as soon as we roll out onto the cold concrete, panting in the frosty air. Summer vacations are punctuated by day trips, the grown-ups driving and Christian and me running to keep pace with the diesel station wagon as it winds its way toward town.

As often as we can slip away; we bolt to the farthest corners of the grounds, where the gardeners haven't cleared away the brush and we can play unburdened by the constant observation of the adults. We build worlds in those branches, full of righteous quests and storybook adventure. When it's raining, we have to resort to hiding places in the house itself, up in the attic mainly, sifting through treasures from my grandfather's travels. We love the mah-jongg set, with its ivory tiles covered in dragons and symbols. In one corner there's a desk, with a typewriter and a ham radio. That's our favorite place. The most sacred place. That's where we spend wet summer days listening to static the way a gypsy peers at tea leaves, trying with all our might to decipher some distant message from the murk. Sometimes, we catch a word. Sometimes, even a sentence. Then we greedily try to respond, hungry to link hands across the current.

"This is England. Over."

Static.

"Do you copy? Over."

Usually more static. But now and then comes a voice from some far-flung corner of the globe.

"England? Hello, England! Pretoria here." Or São Paulo. Or Mumbai.

We take turns, one of us on the radio dials and one of us typing notes, which we pull out of the typewriter at the end of each session and lay with ceremony on the pile from the days before. We cut out newspaper articles about each place we've contacted and tape them to the corresponding sheet. For the first time, I realize that I can actually communicate with the places in my father's newspapers. For the first time, the storybook characters come within reach. It's exhilarating to know that the outside world doesn't just shake us, but we can also shake it. And it's comforting to know that we're not alone, especially when the adults call us downstairs and the games begin again.

Who can do the most pull-ups, my grandmother challenges. Who can eat the most sausages? Christian hates sausages. He deposits one after the next in the fireplace behind us as we pretend to wolf them down. Then my grandmother's eagle eye catches his sleight of hand and she demands that we eat the discarded links in double time, though they're covered in splinters and ash.

The one time my grandmother lets up is during our afternoon walks, when she shuffles from her regular wheelchair into a gigantic orange motorized version, affectionately called the Buggy. It looks like the space-walk chair astronauts use to maneuver around in the film at the Air and Space Museum. It has a joystick, like a Pac-Man machine, that controls little rubber tires with treads on them, like a moon rover. Every day, after lunchtime drinks and before evening cocktails, the grown-ups gather outside the mudroom for our afternoon walk. My grandmother leads the way, the MC of our parade atop her orange float, and Mom walks beside her, dropping bread for the ducks or pulling flowers from passing branches. Depending on who's around, my uncles and aunts stroll with them, followed by we children, Ben and Christian and any other straggling cousins, surrounded by a pack of golden retrievers I pretend are lions.

We make our way over fields and along the river, collecting tadpoles in jam jars and giving them to my grandmother to hold. There's a train that runs along the ridge of the far hill, and we all stop and wave to it in the distance as it passes on its way to London. Sometimes we come across Trevor, the groundskeeper, piling leaves for a bonfire, and Christian and I stand so close we can feel the heat blistering against our cheeks and the smell of woodsmoke hangs in our hair till we get home. My grandmother never makes us run or recite or compete on those walks. In the crisp country air, she is happy. And she lets us be happy, too.

—

Christian and I are up in the attic one day, messing around on the radio, when we realize that downstairs is quiet. Nobody's called us for hours. It's tempting to just stay up there, but then again, silence might mean access to ice cream in the forbidden kitchen freezer. We pad down the back steps and find the grown-ups hushed in a semicircle around the television, watching a news report about the White House. Only it's not the White House in Washington, D.C. It's a different one. In Moscow. And it's surrounded by tanks.

The significance sets in. My dad is in Moscow. That's why everyone's quiet. Why they're all squinting at the screen, like they might spot him in the crowd. He's been working there these last few months, trying to change the law so people can own their own shops.

"Does the government want its shops back?" I ask the adults. They shoo us away, but we plant ourselves in the corner and watch from the floor.

Like all good news media showdowns, this one has heroes and villains. Hero Mikhail

Gorbachev is locked in his house while villain Gennady Yanayev tries to steal control. Gorbachev has been giving people rights, and Dad's been helping him. Yanayev wants to take all those right back. Along with the shops. And the money. And the country.

My mother is trying my dad's hotel, but the lines aren't connecting.

From our corner, we watch as Yanayev's tanks close in on the capitol. The news is spilling into my real world again. Last time that happened, Laura died. I want to shout at the television, run upstairs to send a warning message out on the wire. Anything to change how this is unfolding.

Then suddenly, live on TV, people begin to fill the streets. They wheel out their fruit carts and push empty streetcars into big metal zigzags. They block the path of Yanayev's tanks. Just like the man in Tiananmen Square. They stand with arms linked for Gorbachev and their shops and their rights and my dad. They hold their ground. And the tanks stand down.

By the time Dad gets home, I'm bursting to hear tales about his heroic fight for freedom. He laughs. "The people are the heroes, my dear. I just sat in my Moscow hotel room. Only hardship I faced was the Soviet toilet paper. We'd better open up that market to

Johnson & Johnson." He smiles. "But seeing as you're interested, why don't you come with me sometime?"

It's an invitation into the pages of the newspaper. My heart is in my cheeks.

"Could I?"

"Why not?" he says. And a year later, when I am twelve, Ben and I set out as unaccompanied minors on Aeroflot, the old Soviet airline, with its winged hammer and sickle emblazoned on the carpeted bulkhead wall. It's been a long time since we've shared an adventure, just the two of us.

When we land in Moscow, it's raining and gray. Our dad meets us at the gate and takes us through the VIP passport line.

"What do you have to do to be a VIP?" I ask. Dad rubs his fingers together in the international sign for money. Ben's explained the basics of the Soviet economy to me on the flight over, and bribes don't seem very shared-hammer-and-sickle-ish, but the regular line snakes on for hours and I need the bathroom, so I don't ask any more questions.

It turns out that most of Russia operates the same way. If we want something that's not available on the supermarket shelves, we head to an expensive hotel restaurant. When we want to be allowed to visit a church, we cough up a donation to the Communist Party. And when we want to skip the line to view Lenin's body, we pay for the private tour guide.

Lenin seems smaller than I'm expecting, petite and fragile. The opposite of all the giant buildings and heavy Soviet statues. He looks weak and human and beautiful.

"Think he'd be surprised how things turned out?" I ask Ben as we emerge into the drizzly daylight of Red Square. Groups of women walk toward the market streets, hunched against the wet. They look older than they are.

"Maybe it's not the end yet," Ben suggests. I think about that for a second, then nod. Can't judge a book in the middle, Mom always says.

We learn the ropes of this new world fast, gypsy children that we are, and before long we're running feral around Moscow and St. Petersburg just as we did Washington, D.C., and London. We play tag inside GUM, the old Soviet department store, a giant skeleton of shuttered doors and crystal hallways, empty and echoing, like a dinosaur carcass in the wind. We fashion toy boats out of sticks and umbrella cloth and sail them in the fountains of the Summer Palace. We chase stray cats around the gardens of the Hermitage and learn which black-market money changers have the best rates.

Dad comes with us on outings now and then, but mainly we see him back at home in his flat in the evenings. He moved into the place when he got tired of staying in a hotel, but he hasn't done much with it except line every wall with books. At the little folding table, we drink tea and tell him about our adventures, and he shares stories about the things we've seen or the places we've been. He sounds different from when he talks back home, though. His words don't have the same force. When I say something about helping the people to be free, he guides the conversation a different way. When I mention that I want to see the White House, where the people held off the tanks with their fruit carts, he stops me altogether. He glances around. "Narnia," he says. And I know he means the part where Tumnus is worried about being overheard by the White Witch's spies. "The trees are on her side," I can hear Tumnus warning in my mother's reading voice. I look at the leaves brushing against my dad's window and stop talking.

"Who wants ice cream?" he asks brightly. And we tumble off in search of sweets.

4

That fall, we return to Washington, D.C., as a home base while my dad commutes to Russia. We move into a brick house on the top of a hill near the National Cathedral, and I take the basement bedroom, with its built-in desk for my new computer and its dial-up access to America Online.

I fall in love with the futuristic song of the dial-up modem, like a duet between C-3PO and the static on my grandfather's ham radio. It becomes Pavlovian, that sound and that sequence, the prelude to chat rooms and newsboards from every corner of the globe. It's like climbing out my bedroom window in Westminster, except instead of just Big Ben, I can see the world.

There are stories from London and Moscow and Rome and Agadir. Places I've been and left no longer seem frozen in time but continue to live and breathe in parallel realities alongside my own. I stay up long after the house above me has fallen dark, dizzy at the number of different human experiences playing out in the exact moment that I sit there, peering into the green-tinted light of the screen.

Daytime is less interesting. I've started eighth grade at the National Cathedral School for Girls, a bastion of social grace that seems unbearable after the wild world-wandering of my childhood. I feel like Mowgli stuffed into a whalebone corset. I take to hiding in the library during lunch or in the unmanicured back brush of the cathedral grounds.

In that claustrophobic tightness, there are two bright spots. My English teacher, Ms. Buchanan, who introduces me to Anne Frank and Harriet Tubman and the role women play in combating tyranny. And my computer teacher, Ms. Schopenhuer, who teaches me to communicate with machines. The two weave together in my mind. A woman who can harness a computer, I reason, might be able to resist a tyrant who has harnessed a gun. I start writing my first attempt at a book. It's about a band of female pirates who use computer code to coordinate their raids on evil warlords and free their child hostages.

I'm telling my mother about this master-work one night at dinner while we're eating our spaghetti. She is listening and nodding. Then suddenly, her face goes distant. She stands up, walks into the kitchen, and picks up the phone.

Something's occurred to her about a call she received earlier from a utility company asking about a bill. My father's away in London, so she'd consulted his checkbook and found a recurring entry for a safety-deposit box. Unaware we had such a thing, she'd phoned my dad to ask what it was, and he'd told her it was to keep the kids' passports secure in case of fire. But she could see our passports, all there on the shelf.

"It's Wednesday," he said. "I get home on Friday. If you're so worried about it, you can pick me up at the airport and we'll drive to the bank together. We'll open the box. You'll see it's empty. And you'll feel silly about making such a fuss." She had let it go, made us dinner.

Then all at once, in the middle of my chattering on about pirates and warlords and computer-coded rescues, she stands up and dials British Airways. I listen to her give her name in a blasé voice, as though she's just confirming her husband's travel. And in the pause that follows, I watch her universe crumble.

Dad has booked new flights—London to Paris, the Concorde to New York, a shuttle to D.C., to empty whatever's in the box and get back to London in time to catch his previously scheduled flight home to D.C.

Some sixth sense had struck her at that dinner table. She is broken and vindicated all at once, fierce and suddenly fully grown. She takes us to a neighbor's, then sets off for Dulles to intercept him in the act.

None of us ever finds out what was in the box, not even my mother. My dad doesn't deny that he flew across the world to empty it. Just refuses to share its contents. He asks my mom to forgive him. And having just discovered that she's pregnant, she does.

—

Doomed though they are, my parents press ahead, moving the three of us girls—Antonia, baby Catherine, and me—back to England. London is still a long flight from my father's work in Moscow, and my mother spends most nights on my bedroom floor as I do my homework, playing R.E.M.'s "Everybody

Hurts" on repeat and crying. I find a string of pearls in my dad's drawer and, knowing they aren't my mom's, flush them down the toilet. I surprise myself with how badly I want them to stay together. After all, my dad's traveled for much of my childhood. He throws a whole pot of pasta at the wall one day, and the red splodge stays there, like a giant Rorschach test, the rest of the year. I want to protect my mom so much it aches.

I throw myself into tenth grade at the American School and take refuge among my ragtag tribe of friends. We're all the same brand of gypsy kid, offspring of diplomats and international businesspeople, moved every year from this country to that one, so accustomed to arriving and leaving that none of us is much good at staying still.

I double up on after-school classes—Sanskrit and theoretical physics. I try my first cigarette and get to second base with Vandad Kashefi. He wears a guitar string around his neck and tells me he melted it playing "Stairway to Heaven." I know he's lying, but compared to the lies about bench-pressing I've heard from other boys, it seems like a respectable creative choice.

I wake up one night to what sounds like wailing. It's not my mother this time. It's deeper, more desperate. I sit on the stairs, and for the first time in my life, I hear my father cry. My mom is comforting him.

In the morning, I find out that his little sister had driven to a state park, stopping at a Wal-Mart on the way to buy an apple, a bottle of wine, and a garden hose. She'd parked at a national historical site and toured the grounds. Then driven up to a ridge at sunset, laid out a picnic, eaten the apple and sipped the wine, before fastening the hose to the exhaust, climbing back into her car, and gassing herself to death. She was my dad's only sibling, his baby sister. "I was so busy pretending I was okay," he says to no one in particular, "I forgot to check whether everyone else was."

——

Right after I turn fifteen, we leave London for Morocco and then D.C. Dad doesn't come with us. It's as if a curtain has fallen on the past, and his name is rarely mentioned. He leaves a message on the answering machine to say he's marrying his translator. Mom licks her wounds, begins to date.

I'm back at National Cathedral for my

last two years of high school. My English classroom has a fireplace in it, across the top of which is engraved "Noblesse Oblige." I remember my dad showing us the dairy farm where he worked as a kid—"good, hardworking Americans," he'd said as he watched the farmhands wistfully, "as noble as they come." I'd gotten goose bumps when he said that. But this new idea of nobility is different. There's a darkness to it. As though this kind of nobility isn't earned; it's bought.

The popular kids maintain power the way their political parents do, spending money and keeping up with the trends. One week they wear and think one thing. The next week they wear and think another. The product of constant informal polling. There's no telling who they are deep down, beneath the shifting sands. No sense of what shape their actual bedrock might be.

My history teacher, Mr. Woods, nods solemnly when I hint at how I'm feeling. "Try this," he says, and hands me **Walden**, by Henry David Thoreau. I retreat to a far corner of the cathedral before skimming the first pages. It's about the dignity of hard work and of following your conscience, even if society doesn't agree. I inhale it like a struggling swimmer newly given air. In this world of lunchroom cliques and designer handbags, it feels seditious to even hold in my hands.

When I close the back cover, I press the book between my palms for a minute. Try to feel it. Absorb it. Like it's something sacred. Then I go to the library to see what else this man has written down on paper. I find "Civil Disobedience" and devour that, too. Paint quotes from its pages on my bedroom wall. The idea that our highest duty is not to follow the law but to do whatever we know to be right fills me with calm and hope and awe. This is the Berlin Wall rusher and the man from Tiananmen Square. This is the Russian fruit seller wheeling her cart into the grind of oncoming tanks.

Something about the responsibility to do what is right lends the quiet moments I steal in the colored sun speckles of the cathedral nave a new urgency. I take a fresh interest in the comparative religion course required to graduate. I read Huston Smith's description of each world tradition like an aspiring translator of the Rosetta stone, matching comparable ideas across the different languages in an attempt to divine some universal key.

One day, I hear that Huston Smith is going to give a lecture at the Smithsonian. He has cancer, I know. This might be his last time speaking in D.C. I skip school and take the Metro to the Washington Mall. I stand at the back of the auditorium in my tennis shoes. We are all one, he says. That is the common thread. After a life of studying human religion in every corner of the globe. On the eve of his own death. That is the lesson his work has taught him. From Christianity to Buddhism to the shamanistic traditions of indigenous tribes, every faith deep down teaches that same truth. I can feel what he's saying in my skin.

When I get back to school, my name is on the Daily List. I trudge into the dean's office to receive my Friday detention. But it's worth a hundred detentions to have heard this man share his wisdom.

The next day, my geography teacher tells me I missed the selection of topics for our end-of-year projects. In my absence, she's assigned me the only one nobody else chose: Aung San Suu Kyi and the political situation in Burma.

It takes me a while even to learn how to say her name. But my dad's often warned us not to dismiss people because they have difficult names or unfamiliar clothes. It's like a filter on a photograph, he told us. Doesn't change the shape of what's beneath.

So I say her name until it's familiar in my mouth: Aung-San-Sue-Chee. Daw Suu, her people call her. The lady Suu. Her father, Aung San, is considered the founder of the Burmese nation, uniting the land's many ethnic minorities and negotiating independence from Britain, only to be assassinated in 1947, six months before colonial rule officially came to an end. Suu Kyi was two years old. Fifteen years later, the military staged a coup and took their decades-long vise grip on power. The generals refused to let Suu Kyi's family come home from India, where Suu's mother was serving as ambassador. There, exiled from her country in crisis, Suu pledged she'd return someday to fulfill her father's legacy and free her people from the tanks on their streets. She went to Oxford, worked at the UN, and got married, warning her husband that she could stay with him only until the day the universe called her back to Rangoon. They had two sons, Alexander and Kim, by the time that happened. True to her word, she returned to Burma, amid the student uprising of 1988. She spoke to a crowd of a half million people at the city's Shwedagon Pagoda, sending them out across the country to demand democracy. Within days, thousands of them were dead. The military opened fire into peaceful crowds in every major city. Storm drains clogged with bodies, and streets flooded with blood-tinged rainwater.

The military arrested Daw Suu. Gave her the choice to go home to England and her family or face imprisonment for life. Surrounded by funeral pyres for murdered students, she chose to stay.

She won the Nobel Peace Prize in 1991. But as I get ready to finish high school in the spring of 1998, she sits in Rangoon, detained by the military under house arrest, these seven years later.

I stick a picture of her on my wall and stare at it. There's steel in her eyes, but she wears a flower in her hair. This feminine warrior for peace. I've never seen anything like her before. Softness and strength. One single conscience that's brought an entire army to its knees. I want to hear my calling as clearly as she does hers. I go looking for the voice inside of me. In nature, along the canal, around Roosevelt Island. And at church, the great big yellow sanctuary at the corner of Potomac and O.

Sunday Mass, a tradition in my family, seems less like perfunctory social ritual now and more like a treasure hunt—a jumble of clues that might unlock some inner vault of knowledge if only they're decoded just right. I have the sense that they might arm me with the ability to follow my conscience one day. Or, at the very least, to hear what it has to say.

In immediate terms, the secret I'm most interested in decoding is where I should go to college. It's the first big fork in my road, and it feels like an impossible leap of faith to bear left or right without any visibility of what lies beyond. I've been accepted to the U.S. Naval Academy to study aerospace engineering and Oxford University to study theology and law. One's a life of service and adventure, maybe even a place in NASA's space program. The other's an endless supply of books and questions and ideas.

I graduate high school in a crisp white dress on the lawn of the cathedral, beneath the gentle clink of the flagpole and a clear blue sky. I choose Oxford, but defer my studies for a year. Instead, I sign up for a volunteer trip to the Burmese border to work with the refugees fleeing Rangoon's military machine. Then I take the cash my mom gives me for a prom dress and hand it to a travel agent in exchange for a ticket to Thailand.

5

Camp life is rich in ways rich people aren't. The refugee families sleeping on mats beside me don't object to the giant red millipedes that wriggle inside our clothing overnight. They're too focused on the joy of waking to safety after a lifetime of fear. I never see them waste one ounce of the stale rations they're issued. They outdo one another with creativity in crafting meals from nothing. Monsoon rains and moldy schoolbooks don't dampen their hunger for education. Every adult in camp is determined to get their children into university, to transcend the cramped humidity of their one-room school on stilts.

I start writing little pieces about refugee life and send them to newspapers for consideration. One or two are published in the local expat blogs, and I begin to feel like a journalist.

I take a particular interest in a Burmese dissident writer named Min Zin, who comes to camp to distribute political writings and update the activists living there on the latest democracy news from the border markets outside.

Min Zin was a teenager during the 8/8/88 protests, organizing students inside Burma before dozens of his friends wound up missing or killed. When his name turned up on the military's target list, he went into hiding in an attic in Rangoon. Nine years later, in 1997, he escaped to Thailand. He found himself a mimeograph machine and a few like-minded activists and they started printing **The Irrawaddy,** Burma's democratic newspaper in opposition. He brings copies to camp every so often and to the border markets that dot the riverbanks. He's in his twenties by the time I meet him. Tall and slender, with wire-rimmed glasses. There is something otherworldly in him. A scholar fleeing an army to write his people free.

When I finally find the guts to approach him, I ask if I can write a profile about his work for one of the local papers. He smiles and says, "So you do talk."

He'll take me to see his newspaper in action, he says. But only if I'll wear a blindfold till we get there. He apologizes for the melodrama. After years in hiding, he's not keen to have his new home discovered. Understandable, I say, and I laugh, because it's surreal and because he's so earnest.

I hold on to him on the back of his motorbike, my eyes pressed shut against the checkered cloth he's tied behind my head. I can feel him breathing. The road gets rougher, and it's clear from the smells and the shadows and the sounds that we're in the jungle. It begins to rain.

When we finally stop, and I pull the cloth free, we're both speckled with red mud. My hair is pasted to my face and neck. We're in a cluster of houses on a dirt track, deep under the canopy. I follow Min Zin as he crosses toward a ladder, then climbs up toward a platform on stilts above us. He disappears through the rectangular hole at the top, and when I do the same, I emerge into a bamboo room and it feels like birth. The floor is covered with typewriters and ashtrays. In one corner sits the mimeograph machine. And everywhere, on all sides, there are books. Alexis de Tocqueville and Václav Havel. Democracy and philosophy and logic and ethics. Like the contents of Oxford University's library, pored over, dog-eared, highlighted, and piled ten volumes deep in a treehouse in the jungle.

I meet Ko Moe Thee, a hulking rebel fighter; he is sitting cross-legged on a bamboo mat, smoking a clove cigarette as a cat sleeps in his lap. I meet Ko Ma, a former political prisoner. His face is hollow and his hands shuffle through pictures of his wife. She died in prison, pregnant with their son. The stories are brutal. But the determination to stand up to such an all-powerful evil is electrifying. I return the next week. And the week after that. Until I am there most afternoons, folding papers or looking up quotations.

Min Zin drives me to and from the treehouse, and on the way we stop to meet activists or drop off bundles of the latest edition. He doesn't make me wear the blindfold anymore, but I still hold on to him when the road gets rough. One day, he puts his hand on mine.

That touch is more charged than any of the high school fumbling I've known until now. Tender and erotic and deep and forbidden. He's going to run for office one day. That, we all understand. He's going to return to a democratic Burma and build a future for his people. A relationship with an American girl doesn't figure into that plan. But he kisses me in the soft evening rain, the two of us at the entrance to the camp with water in our hair.

"See you tomorrow?" he asks, and I nod.

We never touch at the treehouse. All day we work amid the others. Every evening, his hand rests on mine as we tumble through the jungle dark. One kiss per night. That is our ration.

A few months into this treehouse life, Min Zin and Ko Moe Thee call everyone into a circle on the floor. There are protests coming: 9/9/99. An echo of the bloody massacre of 8/8/88. We've been marking Burmese banknotes with the upcoming date for weeks, using stamps carved from potatoes, then spending the money in the border markets to silently spread the word. Now Ko Moe Thee poses a question: What if the military shoots into the crowd again? In 1988, there were no journalists there to capture the killing. There is no Tiananmen Square–style photo of what happened in Rangoon. If things go wrong again, he says, we need to be sure the world knows. We need somebody to be there. To bear witness.

Min Zin's eyes hold mine. He is telling me he knows I am going to go and asking me not to and saying that he is proud of me, all at once. The others sense our silent conclusion, and without any discussion, Ko Moe Thee turns to me and asks, "How will you get a visa?"

It's a good question. The Burmese embassy in Thailand has stopped issuing both student and tourist visas in retaliation for international sanctions. But the junta is desperate for revenue, and business visas are still available if you can show proof of legitimate work. Ko Moe Thee is smiling. "Do you have a secret business in Rangoon you haven't told us about?"

"No," I answer. "But I might know somebody who does."

Daryl is a British thirtysomething investment banker and amateur filmmaker I met at a Free Burma conference while I was researching my high school paper. He works for a Japanese firm that invests in Burma. He can't afford to quit, he told me then, but he loathes the idea of making the generals any richer. So he volunteers his filmmaking skills to the Free Burma movement by way of atonement. We talked for only an hour or so. And it was almost a year ago now. But it seems worth a try.

Min Zin drives me to a pay phone in the little town of Mae Sot, right at the jungle's edge. I call Daryl collect. Miraculously, he accepts the charges.

"How would you feel," I ask, after reminding him who I am, "about taking two weeks off work, flying to Thailand, and pretending to be married so we can get into Burma on your business visa and film the regime at work?"

To Daryl's eternal credit, he says yes.

The treehouse crew and I set to work doctoring satchels, so we can film while we're cycling, and buying Bic pens we can take apart to hide film in when we leave. When Daryl arrives, we pick him up at the airport in Bangkok and go straight to Khaosan Road, where a few dollars can buy a forged anything. We pick up a marriage certificate and make our way to the Burmese embassy to apply for a visa. At the desk, we stage a fight for the clerk. "Who wants to spend their honeymoon on a work trip," I complain.

"Who pays the bills?" Daryl shoots back.

The clerk squints at us for a minute. Then he suddenly looks very tired.

"Next window," he says. And stamps our application "Approved."

Min Zin puts us on the plane on the first of September and I can see in his eyes the lived and relived pain of his years in the place I am going. We say our public good-byes, and I feel the private press of his hand against my back. "Remember ABC Café," he tells me. "If things go really wrong, check the bathroom stall at ABC Café."

Daryl and I settle into our plane seats. I'm the only female in our cabin. And the only Westerner, other than Daryl. The steward peers at us from the galley. I channel my inner honeymooner and flick through a magazine without reading the words.

When the aircraft door opens an hour later, the first thing I notice is the smell. The stale wetness of decay. Like a warning against some secret, hidden beneath the surface. It cloaks us as we walk to the terminal, flanked by minders in military dress. It occurs to me that my mom doesn't know where I am. No one knows where I am, except Min Zin and the boys at **The Irrawaddy,** smoking their cigarettes in the jungle. I take Daryl's hand.

There are immigration desks inside, covered by record books, thicker than Bibles, filled line by line with the names of the people who've come before.

The smell follows us indoors.

"You're married," the soldier says, when we get to the front of the line. I think about how I don't know Daryl at all.

"Yes," I say and give my fake husband a kiss on the cheek. The soldier scowls. In his hands, our passports are opened to our visas.

He picks up a fountain pen and copies our information into the book, adding notes we can't read in the looping figure eights of Burmese script. The metal nib scratches against the page. On our left, I watch a businessman pass a soldier his documents. There's money tucked inside.

"Stay with your tour guide," our officer says. We nod, and Daryl holds his hand out for our passports.

"When you leave," the officer says, tucking our lifelines into a file on his right. We stand there for a beat, two small people stripped of our states. "Or you choose to leave now?" he asks and nods at the door we've just come through.

"That's okay, thank you," I say. "One less thing to hang on to, right, darling?"

"We should have gotten a receipt," Daryl says as we make our way to the cavernous luggage hall, littered with railway scales and ashtrays.

"And submit it where?" I laugh. Daryl laughs, too.

A man is walking toward us. He's Burmese, wearing a centaur-like outfit, Western on top, with a blazer and a crisp collared shirt, Eastern on the bottom, with a folded cloth **lungyi** hanging down to his sandals. He introduces himself as our tour guide, and we understand that he is our minder.

We follow the man out the sliding doors to a car. It has blinds pulled down on the insides of the back windows. Through the front windshield, the traffic is mostly mopeds and military trucks. A red billboard reads:

PEOPLE'S DESIRE
- Oppose those relying on external elements acting as stooges holding negative views.
- Oppose those trying to jeopardize stability of the State.
- Oppose foreign nations interfering in internal affairs of the State.
- Crush all internal and external destructive elements as the common enemy.

Around us, on the sidewalks and under corrugated tin awnings, there are children. They lurk behind doors or parents or curtains. They have the look of deer, alert to passing hunters.

We arrive at the government guesthouse, and the tour guide shows us to our room. Teak carvings and golden-threaded bedclothes. I wonder if this is what the generals' houses look like, in this land of empty rice bowls.

The smell is here too, coating the decadence with decay.

We behave like tourists as we secretly await the protesters we hope will flood the streets on September 9. We visit the shimmering sweep of Shwedagon Pagoda, where there are said to be eight strands of hair from the Buddha, where Daw Suu addressed the protesters before they were gunned down. I watch the monks light incense in their saffron robes. Time feels fluid here. On that fateful day—August 8, 1988—this space was filled with noise. The cacophony of college kids, aflame with youth and hope and bluster. Two weeks later, the sounds had turned to wailing. Thousands of families burning their dead. And two weeks after that, these same stones were bathed in silence, the pagoda locked down by Humvees and canvas-covered trucks. The vehicles of the State Law and Order Restoration Council. The SLORC. Like something from Lewis Carroll—the SLORC and the Jabberwock— they sound like monsters too absurd to be real, except one of them is. And in this very place, it bared its claws.

The monks sit straight and passive here, amid all the echoes of the past, drawing on something even the SLORC can't kill. Their faces don't register the rumble of army convoys. I recognize something of the secret they're experiencing. It's familiar, like a scent from my past, the stained-glass dappled stillness of cathedral afternoons.

That evening, in our guesthouse, I can still feel it. The tiles are covered with a thin film of murk. In the corner, under the sink, a spider is eating a centipede. It isn't the sort of place where I'd expect God to hang out. But nonetheless, suddenly and forcefully, God is there.

Daryl comes back from a trip down the hall.

"Our tour guide is wondering if we'd like to enjoy some dinner," he says. I'm growing to like Daryl. He's dry and funny and brave. The world doesn't have many bankers who feel the need to make up for their employers' investment choices with their own love and labor. It has even fewer who manage to do it without bragging.

"Such attentive hosts," I answer. "ABC Café?"

He smiles. "Where else?"

I'm looking forward to leaving a note for Min Zin's network. We've been in-country a few days, and it's time to check whether the system's working.

ABC Café is situated on Maha Bandula

Street, a few blocks from Sule Pagoda and the notorious Traders Hotel, where military officers meet with Chinese drug lords while sipping Singapore slings. The café has the look of an old western saloon, and I like it immediately.

"I'm going to the bathroom," I tell Daryl; he nods on his way to find us a table. Min Zin has told us to leave our notes in the water tank of the toilet. I pull a piece of paper towel out of the dispenser and write a few lines. No identifying information, in case it's intercepted. Just confirmation that we're okay and a request for him to reply so we know the plumbing's intact. I needn't have worried, though. When I lift the porcelain tank lid, there's a scrap of paper already taped there, with an amaryllis flower drawn on the outside. I unfold it and read:

"Order the French fries."

It's like teleportation, having him there with me in the slender strokes of his pen. His characteristic humor. Never one to take himself too seriously. Even in the midst of a full-fledged revolution.

We order fries, as instructed; they arrive with chopsticks and a side of hot sauce. The waiter looks back and forth between us. "You are welcome here," he says, and for the first time since we landed, I know that we are. I can imagine Min Zin here, in the safe energy of secret comrades. His attic—his hidden home for all those years—is a few streets over. It must have been a comfort, once he was stuck there, to know that his underground clubhouse was so near.

We eat in peace, ignoring our minder, whose head periodically pops over the saloon doors to check that we are still where he left us. A singer takes the stage and belts out "Take Me Home, Country Roads." For some reason, it makes me want to cry. Never was a place less wild or free than this military hostage of a town.

Small groups whisper around tables. The music is cover for forbidden conversation. Daryl is watching them, too. We're wondering the same thing, I know. Are they talking about the protests planned for the ninth? Will they still be here to talk about them on the tenth?

We leave the restaurant's glow and step back into the Rangoon night, into the minder's car, and return to the room.

I run my finger against the dresser mirror as I pretend to fix my hair. Min Zin told me that a one-way mirror has no space between your fingernail and its reflection. This one seems fine. But I turn to Daryl with a tinge of mischief.

"Guess they're probably expecting us to have sex. I mean, we are newlyweds, after all."

Daryl laughs. "Get outta here, kid," he says and throws a pillow at me.

It feels good to have addressed it, the nights in a shared bed stretching out ahead of us. With that elephant ushered from the room, I change into pajamas and fall asleep with him beside me, like a guardian in the dark.

We need to clear out of the capital in the lead-up to the protests to avoid suspicion about the reasons for our trip. Travelers used to visit an old fortress town to the north called Mandalay, before the junta shut down the tourism sector to any without a business visa. It makes the perfect diversion, and the next morning we set off for its ancient red stone walls via overnight train.

We buy tickets for a sleeping compartment, where the seats are supposed to slide down their creaking rails to become a long, flat bed. Our seats turn out to be broken, stuck forever upright. But before the rooftops of Rangoon are gone, our minder falls asleep, propped up between the backrest and the window. It's the first time I've been able to take him in, the first time it's felt safe to watch him for longer than a moment. He looks tired, even in rest. I wonder about his family and his choices and the things he grapples with in the quiet of the night. The sting begins to fade from my idea of him. Would I stand up to the military in my own country? Or would I go along to survive, once they proved beyond sufficient doubt that resistance meant death or worse for my mother, my sisters, my father, my brother? I realize in the dimness of the compartment that I have no way to answer. We talk with certainty while our lungs are filled with freedom, but it's harder here, in this suffocating place, to be sure we'd all fight back. At the beginning, maybe, when victory seems possible and it's only our own skin we risk. But after the claw has closed tight around the throats of those we love? Of that I can't be sure. And in the staleness, I feel the minder's despair, choosing between slavery and death.

The window is pitch-black now, as though it's been given the once-over with a tar brush. The train is moving, making its way north, but we can tell only from the jolting of the seats. Outside, there isn't even enough light to sense the passing of shadows. "Guess this is what the SLORC means when it talks about its modern economy," Daryl says, but neither of us laughs. We just stare into the darkness of a nation blacked out from the map, deprived of electricity by the generals who drink beneath the chandeliers of Traders Hotel. Hour upon hour, we watch the darkness pass behind our own reflections. Mile upon mile, I imagine the schoolwork and the cooking undertaken in the void.

We wake to bright sunlight. Children play along the tracks. Their mothers offer food through the windows. Cooked meats and insects on sticks. Juices in tied plastic bags with straws sticking out. One older girl, eleven or twelve, herds her siblings. It looks like she's telling them a story. I watch her as long as I can. She is a glimmer of hope in this place. The first spark of tomorrow I've seen since we arrived.

On the other track, a train passes. There's a flatcar in front of its engine to ensure that any land mine it might encounter won't derail it. And on the flatcar, there are people. Families. Parents huddled with their children and bags. Ready to face death by explosion for the chance to escape the civil war to the north. The junta's fighting half a dozen of these conflicts against indigenous tribes who still resist their rule. They've left torched villages and poisoned rice paddies in their wake.

Soon the Mandalay train station emerges from the city's cooking smoke: more pagodas and white brick, just like the station in Rangoon. More rusting filigree and soft black mold. But the platform has a peacefulness about it as passengers disembark in the gentle morning mist. I wonder if they know, up here, about the demonstration to come. Wonder if they'll risk a repeat of 1988, when the rivers ran with blood.

6

Mandalay looks like Rudyard Kipling's poetry, if the colonists were Burmese and they all drove tanks. The buildings still have their air of imperial indifference. Today they house the junta's offices, no more attuned to the needs of the people than the Brits who came before. It's cooler here than in Rangoon, but the smell of the south is also the smell of the north, the stale air of a country broken by its yoke. The streets are littered with razor wire, looped in circles around black-and-red-striped barricades.

Our hotel is more central here. Our room is an unobserved perch from which to watch the street life pass by, unaware of the outsiders in its midst. The cooking fires burn from dawn till dusk, sending coal smoke up toward us in great, inky fans. Children watch the rumbling of army trucks from the steps of the clock tower in the center of the traffic circle. Across the way, a university building stands empty. All college campuses have been shut since the protests of '88. A nation devoid of future doctors and lawyers because the generals are afraid of youth-fueled dissent.

For the next few days, we trail behind our minder as he takes us to the tourist showpieces. We bide our time before heading back to Rangoon and, we hope, to the protests that will tear down this window dressing for good. On the last day before our train leaves for the south, our minder delivers us to a small boat on the Irrawaddy, the river for which Min Zin's democratic newspaper was named.

"Day trip," he says, and we exchange a look, wondering if "day trip" means "sleep with the fishes." It's not on the tour itinerary, and the dark energy of this place is Orwellian enough to make disappearing two newlyweds sound plausible. We've heard stories of activists disappearing while on government-sponsored tours. At least one of them turned up dead in a prison in Rangoon. This particular boat doesn't look very threatening, though. There's nothing for it but to keep our wits about us and climb in.

It's a traditional wooden river craft, with

room for three or four passengers, propelled by a man standing on one end with a pole. We set off, the man working against the current, his face serene in the heat of the sun. On this little floating island, a good swim from either shore, the junta rests and the four of us are quiet. The pole makes gentle splashes and we pass a singing fisherman. Nobody speaks until finally our pilot presses his weight to the right and propels us toward land. Our minder firms back up.

"Traditional Burmese village," he says as we step onto a wooden dock. Above us, at the top of the sloping bank, a line of people wait in national costume, like the actors at the Epcot Center World Showcase we visited as kids. Behind them, a mock village stands like a film set. There is no sign of daily life, no livestock or litter, just a table covered with lunch. In another country, it would be a mediocre tourist excursion. Here, it is more sinister. Some hundred miles from us begins the trail of smoldering villages that used to look like this one, before the military arrived to tame the tribes who fought them. Karen, Kachin, Karenni, Shan. Ancient peoples who refused the SLORC's rule and paid with their homes and their children and their lives. The thatched roofs here are textbook illustrations of the ones refugees describe being set alight. The rice on our lunch table is a monument to the paddies booby-trapped with mines. The quiet is a reminder of children taken from their homes, girls for soldiers' "comfort," boys to fight and kill. This shiny replica is perfect in every detail, save one. The people here are smiling. It's a North Korea–style propaganda village, and today, we are its guests.

We sit at the table as they describe the food. Who are these people and where do they really live, when they take off their costumes and wearily walk home? The women watch me, then look down when I meet their eyes. On their cheeks they wear **thanaka**, a paste made from tree bark to protect their skin from the sun. Each has applied hers in a different pattern. Dots and circles and swirls. A visual language played out across their faces. We saw **thanaka** in Mandalay and Rangoon, too. It's the only part of this town that feels real, the only glimpse of these women's true selves. The designs hint at this one's pluck, that one's sense of humor.

On the way home, the boatman notices the sun's touch across my nose. He pulls out some **thanaka** of his own and kneels to press a smudge across my forehead, then uses the excess to protect my nose and draw designs across my cheeks. It feels sacred, like an anointing, a welcoming to the fold. The minder does not interrupt, and in the sun-drenched river, the current carries us back to Mandalay.

—

Morning brings a second train journey, back down the same track, and I wonder if there are families riding out ahead of our engine, hoping the flatcar doesn't explode. Tomorrow is the ninth, the morning of truth, the day we hope the students will rise.

We try for dinner at ABC Café. We want to sense the mood. But when we arrive, the saloon doors are stiff and the sign says "Closed." We head back to the guesthouse with empty stomachs on empty roads. It's not yet curfew, but the streets are darker than usual. In the windows above them, the blinds are drawn shut. Soldiers pull barricades from the backs of army trucks. The walkways they block are already deserted.

"They know," Daryl breathes against my cheek as we walk from the car to the guesthouse door. We eat a few stashed saltines and fall asleep in silence.

The following morning, the roads are still

closed, but by the time our minder takes us to town for lunch, the sidewalks are returning to their ordinary bustle and ABC Café is open, albeit quiet and empty. I make a beeline for the bathroom.

"It was over before it began," the note in the toilet says. "Several hundred arrested yesterday. Effective preemptive strike." The handwriting isn't Min Zin's. But the tone and the knowledge of where we would come looking reassure me that it was penned by a friend. "Trip can still be useful. ASSK would like to see you. We'll send a car on the 15th at dawn." ASSK is Aung San Suu Kyi, and the fifteenth is six long days from now. I fold the note and put it back where I found it for Daryl to read while I order us fries.

We came to document the way this junta handles dissent. But how do you film the crushing of an uprising when it's crushed before it rises? There's nothing to record now but the silence.

The morning of September 15 dawns streaky gold on the eastern shore of Inle Lake, and we wait outside our guesthouse, as instructed by the toilet tank note. At five a.m., it's still early enough that our minder hasn't yet arrived at our hotel. Neither has the contact we're awaiting. "Maybe they were arrested," I say when the road is still empty a few minutes later. "Maybe the SLORC knows about us the way it knew about the protests." The thought chills me. But then a car grinds out of the dust and stops beside us. We climb inside, and I see the hotel night manager dial his phone as we pull the car door shut.

We set about checking our things. We have our camera and the Bic pens we brought to hide the film. We have our notebooks with cryptic reminders of the questions we want to ask. We have our tools to inquire and record. But that is all. Our passports are back at the airport. Our bags are still in our room. It's terrifying to defy the rules of this ruthless regime with no protection except a bag of film and pens. Nevertheless, we're in the car now. We've crossed the Rubicon. And there's no choice but to plunge into the unknown.

The meeting is at Suu Kyi's party's head-quarters, the only place she's allowed to go outside her home. Its plain brick façade looks more like a storefront than a hive of resis-tance. Only a flag bearing the silhouette of a peacock gives away the building's fiery true purpose. The fighting peacock is the symbol of Burmese democracy: fierce gold against a blazing background of red, one claw raised in preparation for battle. The flag hangs in the second-story window, across from the army's observation post, like a matador's cape to a bull.

It doesn't look like the soldiers have stirred yet this morning. There's no motion as we pull up. Their cooking coals are cold. Our car crawls down an alley, and we climb out into the dawn. The stagnant smell lingers, but a slight breeze stirs the dust.

"This way." The driver is out of the car and shuffling us toward a side door. Still no response from across the street. We're not used to roaming this city freely. It doesn't feel as good as I'd imagined. When the minder is with us, the threat has a form. Without him, it becomes a nebulous, all-powerful force. Empty doorways and shapes among the shadows.

When we get to the door, I press down on the latch and it opens. Locks are just window dressing here. The soldiers will come and go as they please. I admire Daw Suu's party for not bothering with the game of pretend.

The ground floor is an unfurnished space, open to a rickety balcony above. On the wall is a picture of Suu Kyi speaking at the balcony's edge to a packed crowd of supporters below. But today, it's only us.

"Please," the driver says and motions for us to climb the stairs. At the top, beyond the balcony, is a narrow hallway. He overtakes us and knocks on the door. After a beat, it opens.

She is smaller than I expected. She has no entourage, no security. She stands on the wooden threshold, welcoming us into an empty room. Her hand fits in mine like a child's.

"Please come in." Her accent is British with a colonial residue, the kind that is still taught in the private schools of Mumbai. Her posture is immaculate, every bit as disciplined as the soldiers across the road. In her hair, she wears flowers, just as she did in the photo on my high school bedroom wall. Just as in that picture, there is steel in her eyes. And here in person, I see that somewhere under the steel, there is love.

"Thank you for seeing us," Daryl offers.

"Any friend of Min Zin's," she says, and when she smiles, the room warms.

We sit at the long wooden table while Daryl unpacks the camera. There are bars on the window.

"If you get this film out," she says, "ask a news outlet to broadcast it back into Burma on shortwave, so it can't be blocked. We won the elections almost ten years ago, but still it's impossible for people outside of Rangoon to hear what I say."

Over the hour that follows, she talks about the economy, human rights, the cleansing of ethnic minorities. She condemns slave labor at the nation's gas pipelines and the drug trade that enriches the elite. Years from now, she will face accusations of abandoning these same people, but in this room, on this day, she is fierce and resolute.

She says Burma was known as the rice bowl of Asia, before Ne Win, the head of the military, decided that nine was his lucky number. Overnight, he voided all currency not divisible by nine. With no banking system, families kept their savings in hundred-kyat notes, stashed away in their homes. Burma's wealth was wiped out. Having been one of Southeast Asia's richest nations, it quickly became the poorest.

Ne Win bathed in dolphin blood to stay young and did as his soothsayers told him. One night he ordered the main thoroughfare in Rangoon shut down so he could walk across a bridge backward, dressed as an emperor. Behind the scenes, he bought his power by paying the generals millions of dollars via bank accounts in Switzerland—using the profits from turning a blind eye to trade in humans and drugs.

When the students objected to the rape of their country, Ne Win ordered those same generals to shoot into crowds from Rangoon to Mandalay. Those were the protests of 8/8/88, when Suu Kyi took on her father's mantle and Min Zin was driven to his hideout in the attic. Thousands were killed, and Suu Kyi was placed under house arrest. Eleven years later, she still can't leave her home except to visit the very building in which we are sitting, its door guarded by the soldiers across the street.

Before we finish the interview, she describes the villagers forced to work as slaves along the pipelines that make the generals rich. She tells us about volunteer lawyers from America who have found a hundred-year-old law, written to prosecute pirates for crimes on the high seas. They think they can use it to hold the California-owned gas company accountable, maybe even the generals, too. The lawyers may have to take it all the way to the U.S. Supreme Court. They are going to fight for Burmese villagers half a world away.

I'm mesmerized, listening to this tiny woman tell me the ways nonviolence in the streets and the courts can deliver a ruthless military to its demise. But for now, she's still under house arrest. She hasn't defeated the junta yet.

In order for her words to make it farther than the open room downstairs, we have to take the film apart and hide it. While we unscrew the plastic casings, Suu Kyi talks about her husband, Michael, an Oxford professor of Tibetan Studies who died of cancer a few months ago. Her two boys, still school-aged, are without either parent now. The military will let her leave Burma anytime she chooses. She could have gone to Michael's bedside before he passed. She could go now to hold their grieving children. But she knows that if she leaves, she will never be allowed to return. I imagine being one of her sons, in the quiet of an English country house, with newspaper clippings instead of a mother. I wonder if they are more resentful or more proud. I think of my own father in Russia and his empty seat at my high school graduation.

When the film is liberated from its plastic, I begin to thread it into the pen casings. Suu Kyi puts her hand on mine. "Those are fine for the decoy film," she says. "The scraps you want them to find so they think they've gotten it all." Then gently, like a patient god-mother, she adds, "For the real footage, the film you actually want to get out, nature has given you a better hiding place." She rolls the film of our interview into a cylinder smaller than a tampon and seals it in plastic wrap. She hands it to me and says, "The bathroom is down the hall on the left."

When we walk out the front door, fifteen minutes later, the soldiers are awake and at their post. We can hear the metallic clicking of a camera shutter snapping our departure. Neither of us turns to look. We walk toward the main road, where Suu Kyi has told us we can catch a taxi if the soldiers let us leave.

The film concealed inside me contains more than just comments on the economy and civil wars. It contains a rallying cry for the people of Burma, a plea not to give up, a demand that they rise again. These are the most seditious words Suu Kyi has uttered in some time, provoked by the preemptive jailings last week. And it's our responsibility now to make sure those words are heard.

"There's a taxi," Daryl says. But before we can reach it, a military pickup truck pulls up beside us and a man with a gun says, "Get in."

Min Zin has warned us: If soldiers engage us, we're to be meek and obedient. No flashy resistance or moral outrage.

"Your victory will be getting out of there,

hopefully with footage intact," he told us. "Don't do anything to jeopardize that goal, however tempting it might be to spit at their feet."

We climb into the back of the truck, and the soldiers lace the canvas closed behind us. I can feel my pulse in my fingertips, and everything slows down, the way a car accident feels right before you hit.

Even though there's no one in the back with us, instinctively, we do not speak. I try to keep track of the turns. After a few minutes, I give up.

When we stop and the driver cuts the engine, we can still hear the sounds of city traffic. They haven't taken us too far. Certainly not far enough to reach Insein Prison or any of the detention centers outside of Rangoon. Relief prickles my arms like rain.

We hear the soldiers get out of the cab. A minute later, the canvas opens. We are outside a strange hotel. "Get your things," the taller soldier says.

"This isn't our hotel," Daryl replies.

The two soldiers talk between themselves for a moment, in Burmese. Then they close the canvas again and return to the driver, who's waiting up front. The truck lurches back into motion. Were they buying time?

Was it a genuine mistake? What will happen after we pick up our things? Daryl holds my eye. He's telling me it's going to be okay.

We pass the temple sounds of Sule Pagoda. Then the cries of the vendors at Aung San Market. Two weeks ago, I'd never been to this city. Now I can feel my way through its streets by sound. Beyond the canvas are monks and merchants and militants and mothers. All victims of one madman with a gun. In some way I can't explain, I've come to love them. I wonder if the children at the tea stalls are watching our truck pass beside their games.

We stop again, and when the canvas opens, we are in the driveway of our hotel. Daryl smiles his dry British smile.

"Get our things?" he asks. The tall soldier nods. He's annoyed by Daryl's show of humor. But that small joke reminds me that we are still ourselves. I squeeze Daryl's hand as we lead the men to our room.

The first thing they do is collect all the money they can see. Then they ask us if we have any more, and we produce a few rumpled notes. The shorter soldier holds up the pile without counting it.

"Exit tax," he says.

I can see the pens with the decoy film,

tucked in my satchel pocket. I can feel the actual film inside my body. I wonder if they'll search us. But instead they hustle us back into the truck and throw our luggage in beside us. I listen for the sounds of Shwedagon Pagoda and Inle Lake, which we'll pass on the way to the airport. Each comes on time and I check them off in my mind, small comfort by small comfort. Then the canvas is drawn back a third time, and we are not at the terminal.

The airport is nearby, although from what I can tell of our surroundings, so is Insein Prison. The building beside us looks like a cross between the two—an airplane hangar with razor wire around its perimeter. My calm evaporates. I try to tell myself that it's possible we're on a charter flight or that we're being held separately from the normal passengers to ensure that we don't make a scene. But then a prisoner is pulled from a van near our pickup and escorted inside with a rag tied over his face and his hands bound by cord. One arm hangs limp from his shoulder, as if only his skin is holding him together. I feel for Daryl's hand, but he is ahead of me, being pushed toward the door.

The soldier beside me prods me to follow. Inside, there is a tall table, around which a few officers are huddled. A dozen or so children in military uniforms sit on the cement floor. The bound man is not there. I eye the metal door he must have passed through. What is this place? And will we ever leave it?

The soldiers direct us to sit on two low plastic stools. The short one crouches between us, while the tall one walks over to the table and lights a cigarette.

We are there for some hours. I watch the boy soldiers play jacks. They are nine or maybe ten years old, wearing miniature uniforms with tiny epaulets on their shoulders. One smokes a cheroot, a type of Burmese street cigar sold on every corner. He taps ash into a soda bottle. Against the wall and cradled in laps, there are guns, one per boy, taller than their child owners, if you count the bayonets. Game after game, they play without cracking a smile. Their bodies move through the motions. Their eyes have the glassed-over distance of narcotics and loss.

Officers come and go. Sometimes, they shout. Mostly, they shuffle papers. One prods a new prisoner across the room and through the far door without stopping. Now and then there is a cry of pain from beyond the door. After one, a soldier turns to us and grins. "Car battery," he says, and I don't know whether to believe him. I remember my uncle attaching jumper cables wrong when I was little, producing a little burst of sparks. I wonder how much it would hurt to channel that voltage through my body. I wonder if I'd scream.

A few hours after that, we're taken through the door. A beige-tiled hallway stretches to the left and right. We're separated, put into rooms, and the doors are locked. It happens in an instant. One moment we are together, and the next, I am alone in the universe.

The room is empty except for a chair and a pot. No bedroll. No mat. No sign that this place is designed for long-term holding. I walk a circle around the cell for a long time. Then I sit down in the middle of the floor and close my eyes. I try to tell my family where I am. I try to tell Min Zin that I'm okay. I ask God that they not rape me.

Every so often, the silence is punctuated by another cry, of cruelty or of pain.

After what seems like days but I learn later was less than twenty-four hours, a soldier opens the door and stands there until I understand I'm supposed to go with him. We walk back to the main room. Daryl is there, and so are our passports. The remnants of our luggage are piled on the floor. The pens are gone. The lining of every bag has been slashed. An officer I haven't seen before is scribbling something across our visas; then he closes our passports and hands them back to us. My vision blurs for a second. I press back tears. Of relief. And of sorrow for the bound men left behind.

Outside the hangar door, it is the last dark before dawn. There are more trucks now, empty of their prisoners and piled with weapons like abandoned toys. I take them in, the trucks and the guns and the razor-wire barricades. All this violence and might to silence some college kids with slogans and signs. All this orgy of force just to keep one woman from speaking her truth. I can feel Suu Kyi's words tucked inside me, and I know that today the soldiers have failed.

—

When we land in Bangkok, Min Zin is waiting for us, along with Ko Ma and a few others from the treehouse. Their eyes dance as we get off the plane. There is an electricity around us, a sense of having fought back the darkness. Min Zin leads us to a restaurant with trees growing out of the floor, and we drink unnaturally colored cocktails while he asks us about the interview and the soldiers and the airplane hangar with razor wire around its perimeter. Story by story, we alternate between exhilaration and despair.

The next morning, we set about keeping our promise to Suu Kyi, knocking on the door of the BBC's Radio Bangkok and asking if they'll broadcast the interview back into Burma on shortwave. They square us up for a minute, detecting both our hubris and our good intentions. "Sure, let's give it a go," a young Aussie says. We reconstruct the film with their technicians and listen to the first recording of Suu Kyi's voice heard outside Burma for almost a year.

Not long after the BBC broadcasts the interview, CNN calls me and asks for comment on how Suu Kyi's words are affecting morale in Rangoon. Min Zin tells me about his years in hiding and how much it meant to him each time he heard a fresh rallying cry, proof that the resistance was alive beyond his makeshift prison walls. I picture the resistance fighters still holed up in attics and basements and storerooms a few hundred miles across the border. I imagine the fuel this radio broadcast might offer them. For the first time in my life, I feel the high of not just observing the world but actually changing it. I want to stay in the moment forever. But September is almost gone. Oxford is about to begin. And my mother is worked up with worry, ever since she learned of our detention. There's no option but to go home.

Min Zin kisses me good-bye at the airport. I watch my beloved jungle recede out the airplane window and, with it, the first version of myself that feels real.

7

I turn up at Oxford wearing a **lungyi** and Burmese flip-flops. I'm an awkward outsider in this stronghold of Britishness, and I keep the memories of Min Zin and Tocqueville close. I hide in my dorm room and talk with editors at CNN.

I chose Oxford to take advantage of its renowned international law program, to follow in the footsteps of Suu Kyi and Min Zin and one day do my part to challenge tyranny on behalf of the powerless. But the pondering lectures make me feel more like I'm in a socialite's salon than a forge for the warriors of freedom. Each week, I write my required essay and trudge to my tutorial—a one-on-one session with this or that brilliant and eccentric professor, beginning with the offer of sherry and snuff and ending with the strong suspicion that nothing we've just discussed applies to the real world. At night, I pull on my billowing academic gown and shuffle to the dining hall, with its cathedral ceiling and gallery of oil paintings suspended between stained-glass windows speckled with rain. I sit alone amid the riches and long for the low, plastic stools of Burmese tea stalls and the makeshift meals of Min Zin's tree-house floor.

A few months into this period of all but hibernation, an older student knocks on my door and introduces himself as Emmett Fitzgerald, my college "grandfather," explaining that a third-year student is traditionally assigned to each first-year to guide them through the university's mess of ancient rules and customs. He's Irish and recklessly handsome, with a smile that brings out innuendo in a joke the way air brings out flavor in wine. It's pretty clear that in the Venn diagram of Oxford cliques, our circles would not have naturally overlapped. But we take to spending evenings in my room, indulging in the obligatory philosophical debates of college dorms everywhere: Are plants conscious? If you could save your sister or a thousand strangers, which would you choose? Is this all a simulation? In my room, we are equals.

Outside its door, he's a rower and I'm not anyone at all. He dates pretty girls and I stay home.

Our evening rambles through philosophy and laughter tap a hole in my armor, and I begin to consider the possibility of making friends. I meet Anthony, a soft-spoken South African whose dad owns a teddy bear shop and whose mom is a schoolteacher. He's gentle and funny and an outsider like me. The night we spend together becomes two and then three, until before I know it, we are one another's shadow. He's not Min Zin but he doesn't try to be, and in this removed kingdom of spires and stone, we find shelter in each other's care.

He takes me to drink Pimm's at the boat races and dance in costume at masquerade balls, but my memories of Burma turn from a source of comfort to a source of dismay. How can we swank around parties while the Burmese junta is killing students like flies? Anthony tries to make me laugh. He takes me to our college bar, where the idiocy of drinking games sends me deeper into the dark. Then one night, I drink too much of the whiskey he's left in my room. I write him a letter to explain how it hurts too much, feeling the world. Then I slice open my left wrist.

It bleeds more than I would have guessed, red across my homework. I watch the blood expand in circles across my law-book pages. I think of Min Zin and the years he spent in the silence of an attic to escape a death sentence so that he could fight for his people. And then I realize that I'm an idiot.

I grab a washcloth and hold it hard against my wrist, run downstairs and out the door to find help. By the time I'm stitched up and home, Anthony's waiting for me in my room. The next morning, he tells me that when he arrived and saw my note covered in blood, then read my rambling description of pain hitting me like a train, he thought I'd set off to jump in front of one, and he called the police to have every train in Oxfordshire slowed to five miles per hour.

Emmett comes to visit. Looks the blood-crusted letter over with his blue Irish eyes. Then turns to me and says, "Y'know, kiddo, you need to learn some kung-motherfuckin'-fu. You feel the world and it just socks you, right? Wham! Harder than most people. Well, sure, if you take the force of that punch, it's gonna get you every time. But now, you see, kung fu masters, they can take the force that's coming at them and throw it right into their next move. Harder they get hit, the stronger their game. Master that kung fu, and you've got yourself a superpower, kiddo."

The next week, I pass an Amnesty International flyer on my way through the quad. I rip off one of the phone numbers and stick it in my back pocket. By the end of the year, I'm humming in sixth gear—writing about human rights for the school newspaper, planning debates at the Oxford Union, organizing campaigns for student office, raising funds for prisoners of conscience. Slowly, I stop seeing myself as a sponge, soaking up suffering till it drowns me. And I start seeing myself as a converter, metabolizing suffering into action.

—

During my second year, I find a note in my mailbox asking me to meet a professor at the Fuggle and Firkin, a pub in central Oxford, for a drink. We sit upstairs on a green velvet sofa: him, me, and two former students of his—men in their twenties, who ask about my travels in Thailand, about my experience with the junta in Burma. I seem set on making the world a better place, they tell me. Have I heard of a group called al Qa'ida? I know the name, from the Africa bombings

and the USS **Cole.** How about the Taliban?
Yes, I saw their strange press announcement,
I say, before they blew up the giant Buddhas. I
comment on how young the Taliban fighters
seemed, almost as if they could be here at
Oxford, in a different life. I talk about how
I'd tried to see into their eyes through the
TV. They look at one another and smile.

They ask if I've given any thought to what
I'll do after university, and I tell them yes,
in fact, I've been offered a job working with
refugees in Southeast Asia. They nod politely
and ask if they can suggest an alternative;
they explain that they need people like me,
to help them learn more about the Taliban,
about al Qa'ida, about the threat extremists
pose. They talk about how most people don't
understand how quickly civil society can
fall apart, but I do, don't I, having lived out
"there," by which I sense they mean somewhere beyond the realm of rules about your
salad fork. The more they talk, the less I like
them. They ask me if I'll think about helping them. I've been breaking into foreign
regimes already, after all, so why not do it
for them? They talk about the importance of
secrets, and I think about my dad's safety-
deposit box and my mom on the floor of my
bedroom listening to "Everybody Hurts."

I tell them, "I don't believe in your

cloak-and-dagger stuff." I say, "Thanks for the pint."

I never hear from them again. Never find out what flavor they were—MI5, MI6, GCHQ. I see the professor at high table in our college dining room from time to time.

That spring, I'm asked to be a guest liaison for the Oxford Union, the university's famous debating society. The job entails meeting guest speakers at the airport or train station and transporting them to their hotels, then taking them out for supper to run them through the schedule for the following day. I fall in love with the rhythm and passion of debate, the principle of equal time for opposing opinions, the assumption of respect for every person who stands before the house, regardless of their background, so long as their ideas are sound. It is Jeffersonian and noble, the sort of thing described and underlined in Min Zin's books in the jungle. I find it electrifying, following the politics of the Union presidential bids, until Anthony decides to run for treasurer and the Jeffersonian nobility gives way to sausage-making and backroom deals. I learn the endless variety of ways that small-print rules and regulations can be used to override the voice of voters. Here in this cauldron of hubris and potential, aspiring politicians and lawyers raise competing points of order to ensure that some arcane strategic advantage be awarded to their slate of candidates. Showboats and loophole hounds prevail. By the time the game is over, the next round is already ramping up to be played, with candidates for next term's offices whispering over their pints in the pubs down the road. Between rounds of play, there's no time left to govern. The real service is done in the back office by unnamed employees and volunteers with pencils in their hair.

Anthony and I escape the power games to spend the summer of 2001 in Bosnia, working with kids left orphaned by the Srebrenica massacre. I'm twenty and it's my first time living in the immediate aftermath of war, the first time I witness the way violence rewires young minds. The kids one-up one another about how violently their dads were killed, the way American kids fight over whose dad has better tickets to the Broncos game. "My dad's eyes were gouged out with a spoon," one boy tells me proudly. They bring knives to school. They throw stones at the Croatian kid, who happens to be a six-year-old girl. But somewhere underneath that, they remind me of my sisters, now six and thirteen, and I ache for what they've seen. The last night, we hold a slumber party in the youth center's gym, piling blankets and pillows on the basketball court. The six-year-old Croatian girl climbs into my lap and falls asleep, while one of the big kids confesses that he's scared he's inherited the violence of his father. On the train back to England, I write to the Thai refugee camp and accept the job for after graduation.

—

I go home to visit my mom and sisters in Washington, D.C., before my last year at Oxford begins in the fall of 2001.

I'm sitting on the steps of our house in Georgetown, sipping coffee and watching my mom walk Sam, our golden retriever, in the park across the street. Our neighbor pulls up at the stop sign. He has the top of his Volkswagen Rabbit down. His face is white. "Turn on the news," he says. And I switch on the TV just before the second plane hits.

My sisters are at school on the grounds of the National Cathedral, so once Flight 77 plows into the Pentagon, their campus is evacuated. Mom and I put Sam in our Jeep and fight through gridlock to get to them, while the radio tells us we're at war and the black plume of smoke from across the Potomac expands across the sky. "Let's get out of D.C.," I suggest, once we have both girls, "till we understand what's going on." So we drive to a suburban Denny's, the only place left open, and watch the news on the TV there. My head is swimming. We're at war. I look at my sisters in their school uniforms, with their hair in neat braids—and I remember the kid back in Bosnia, with the dad and the spoon and the eyeballs.

Lisa, my childhood friend from London, is living in D.C. by now, and the following day we drive up to New York City, just the two of us in her beaten-up truck. We have no reason to go. It's just instinct, like putting your finger to a wound. We can see the smoke from the New Jersey Turnpike. When we get to the tollbooth at the mouth of the Holland Tunnel, Lisa realizes she's forgotten her wallet and begins to cry. The woman inside the window begins to cry, too. She waves us through.

Across the river, the downtown streets are dusted gray, like the pictures of Hiroshima in my high school history books. Every lamppost, every wall is covered with flyers, each with a person's face and the word MISSING in capital letters, like a howling, hopeless prayer. We walk south through the ash.

A few blocks from ground zero, the road is closed and we can't go any farther. Neither of us has spoken in hours. We look at each other, then at the firefighter manning the barricade. "What can we do?" I ask, and he points us to a water station where bottles need unpacking. Shift after shift, the emergency workers come and go in suits and respirators with horror in their eyes. One of them picks up a red tennis shoe and stares at it, while the others work around him.

When I get back to Oxford, time and again, I wake up swearing I smell smoke.

—

In January, Danny Pearl gets kidnapped in Karachi.

Danny's been a writing hero of mine for a couple of years now. I scarcely know him, but we've crossed paths a few times—in D.C., while I was still in high school and he was just starting out at **The Wall Street Journal**, and later in Southeast Asia, as I began to cut my teeth and he offered gentle advice on my stories. I'd always been amazed by his easygoing strength of character, an Israeli-American writing compassionately about life in Pakistan. Now he's bound with a gun to the back of his neck, while his wife—pregnant with their first child—and colleagues work frantically to find him.

He was researching a story on Richard Reid, the Englishman who stuffed his shoes with explosives and boarded an American Airlines flight from Paris to Miami three days before Christmas. Danny had a lead. A cleric close to Reid had agreed to meet him at a restaurant in Karachi. When Danny arrived, he was told that the meeting had been moved for security reasons, hustled into a car, and driven into the Pakistani dark.

Then the pictures start appearing: Danny holding newspapers with fresh dates beneath their mastheads and chains around his wrists.

He's the **Wall Street Journal**'s South Asia bureau chief, and I take comfort in imagining the paper's agents working behind the scenes to buy his safe return. The proof-of-life photos are right off the pages of the kidnapping thrillers they sell at the airport, the kind where ransoms get paid and heroes get home before their babies arrive. But days turn to weeks with no word of his release.

Four weeks after the first picture, I walk into our grubby subterranean college bar. I've got a winter cold and ask Len, the barman, to make me a hot toddy. On the rabbit-eared TV, the crawl type says Danny's been beheaded. I feel winded, like I've taken a soccer ball to the gut.

In the days that follow, the media outlets play excerpts of the video showing Danny's head being sawed off his body. The experts argue over whether the hand that did it belongs to al Qa'ida. They show Danny reciting words he was made to memorize, words as far from his compassionate worldview as can be. I can't watch. I go for dawn walks in the meadows by the river—the same meadows where J.R.R. Tolkien and C. S. Lewis wandered while discussing Christianity. I ask God out loud to help me understand what is happening and what I can do with my life to make it stop.

In Thailand, I'd be able to throw myself into the familiar, to pretend that the world isn't being swallowed up by this new kind of war. But the more I walk, the more deeply I realize that hiding won't help me. I'm going to be afraid of what's happening until I can answer the question "Why?"

I apply to a master's program in conflict and terrorism at Georgetown's School of Foreign Service. When I get accepted, I call the Thai NGO and tell the director that I'm not coming.

—

As soon as I get to Georgetown, I put a little plastic bat on my desk to remind me of the time my dad helped me take apart my brother's toy vampire bat to understand how it worked. I'd woken my parents up crying because the bat had been in my dreams, and so my dad had sat with me on the floor and pulled open the bat's belly. We'd laid out all the pieces: the battery that made his eyes glow green and the little red rectangle of felt that swirled around inside his giant plastic proboscis to give the look of sucked-up blood. After that, I'd never been afraid of him again.

When it comes time to choose a thesis topic, I decide to give terrorism the vampire bat treatment, take it apart and lay it out on a table. I dig up two hundred years of data on every attack, domestic and international, and look for unnoticed patterns—things like the ratio of hookah bars to madrassas and the percentage beneath livable wage a border guard gets paid. I weigh each factor based on past impact and string them all together into one algorithm, so you can plug in data for any region and, bazam, it spits out the probability that the area will be used as a terrorist safe haven against its will.

It turns out that Georgetown has a CIA officer in residence, a Santa Claus look-alike named Dallas Jones, and this algo piques his interest. He asks me whether I'll talk with his colleagues. And this time, because of his kind eyes, maybe, or his earnest desire to understand humans, I say yes. I like the group of people he introduces me to. Unlike the men back in Oxford, they are curious and humble and genuinely interested in questions that begin with "Why."

They ask me how I found the data I used, and I show them my endnotes. They ask me if I feel like I got all the inputs. Of course not, I tell them. I'm missing the most important input of all: sitting with a cup of tea across from someone who trusts me enough to tell me why he's planning to fly a plane into a building. "That's what I wish I understood," I say.

They say, "So do we."

They give me the address of a hotel in Arlington and a date and time to be there. And so begins a long process of interviews and current affairs exams, recruitment role-playing and language aptitude tests, psych batteries and polygraph machines. Finally, at twenty-two years old, I receive a provisional offer of employment at the Central Intelligence Agency. If I accept, they'll still have to process me for security clearance, and given my international background, it's anyone's guess if I'll pass.

Throughout the process, I confide in no one except my friend Jim, a fellow Georgetown School of Foreign Service student who's also applying. Together we lick the envelopes for our security forms. "Well, now they have a DNA sample," we laugh. We talk about the ethics of this world we're wading into. Promise to hold each other accountable. He gives me a coin that says, "Speak truth to power." I put it on my desk, next to the bat.

We decide to use the summer while they're processing our clearances to take a long trek through Southeast Asia, stopping first in London to visit Anthony. We're a year into trying our hands at a long-distance relationship, but as a foreign national, he can't know anything about applications to join the CIA. It's a tense evening's reunion. He senses secrets in the air and assumes that Jim and I are lovers. I tell him we're not, try to explain away the awkward conversational pauses and cover-ups every time the talk veers too close to my prospective work, but he doesn't believe me and we part ways in tears.

"You're a terrible liar," Jim says to me. "Might want to work on that."

We hitchhike down the Mekong on a fishing boat, befriend homeless kids on the beach in Cambodia, take the night boat from Thailand to Penang. We arrive in East Timor on the first day of its official freedom from Indonesia, and since the government hasn't yet made the new passport stamps, the customs guy writes, "Hari Merdeka Timor Leste" in each of our passports with a ballpoint pen—Independence Day, East Timor. We stay in a shipping container on a boat in the harbor because the fighting has left Dili without any hotels. The presidential palace is missing its top floor, and a cow wanders across its front walk. We get the guard chatting about the reconstruction, and he furtively gives us a look at the architectural plans for the new presidential compound, security infrastructure and all.

"Amazing what people will show two back-packers," Jim comments as we walk away.

That night, we sit on a concrete dock beside a loud, dented generator, our feet hanging over the water and empty beer bottles between us. "That guard looked at us and saw clueless backpackers," I say. "Anthony looks at us and sees star-crossed lovers. Washington looks at us and sees sophisticated spies. Our parents look at us and see kids who still leave laundry on the floor. Do you ever wonder who the fuck we actually are?"

We're silent for a beat. Then Jim scoops up our empties and says, "We're two people in desperate need of beer."

—

The week after we get back to Washington, my grandmother dies. My mom drives to Jim's house to tell me, but she can't. She just sits in the driver's seat of her Jeep, her face shining wet, mouthing words I can't understand, as if the pain is drowning her. I fly to Europe with her for the funeral, stand beside her as we view her mother's body, small and stiff and pale in its wooden box on a black crepe stand. Afterward, Christian and I smoke cigarettes behind the garage. "I wasn't the kid she wanted when she signed those adoption papers," he says. "But she loved me for letting her pretend I was."

I get home to a cryptic voice mail from an unidentified number and return the call to hear that my security processing is complete. I now have top secret clearance with access to sensitive compartmented information, or TS/SCI, meaning that I'll be privy to programs so closely guarded, even the top secret crowd can't see them. I'm to report to CIA headquarters on Route 123 in Langley, Virginia, the following week and, in the meantime, to tell anyone who knows I was applying that I haven't made the cut.

I meet Jim for drinks. I look him in the eye and I lie.

"Yeah right, I bet they just told you to say that," he says.

I start to cry. "I wish," I say.

He seems taken aback. He's never seen me cry. He comforts me. Believes me. But I'm not crying to make him believe. I'm crying because I've lost the last friend who knows my truth.

8

From now on, everyone I love—my mom, my family, my friends—all think I'm consulting for a multinational company, using the algorithm I developed to help its leadership steer clear of instability overseas. It's a temporary training cover, to be replaced by something more permanent if I actually make it through the grueling months ahead. Until then, I'm ostensibly working a mediocre Beltway consulting gig while I finish up my master's at Georgetown. The job explains my distraction, my busy schedule, my periodic absences. And it's boring enough to ensure that nobody asks too many questions.

When I report to headquarters (HQS) the following week, I run my hand along the section of the Berlin Wall in the parking lot as I walk from my car. I stop to read the inscription under the statue of Nathan Hale outside the main door: "I only regret that I have but one life to lose for my country." Inside, I walk across the giant marble seal and stop at the wall of stars, one for each officer killed in the line of duty. I trace the one lost on the same Pan Am flight as Laura. Across from them, carved into the wall between two flags, is scripture: "And ye shall know the truth and the truth shall make you free."

I check in with the desk officer, a middle-aged woman with a cardigan over her uniform and a hint of sass in her smile. There are two sets of folders in front of her. Some are blue, with names on them, and others black, without. "Clandestine service trainee?" she asks me.

"What's that?" I ask, and she smiles.

"If you were one, you'd know," she says and pulls my folder. It's blue.

I eye the black pile, like the second-class citizen I now know I am.

"Black folder's where it's at, huh?"

"Put it this way," she says. "You see the size of the parking lots on the way in here? All those thousands of people come into these buildings every day for one reason: to support **them.**" She taps the black folders. "Either to get them overseas safely, to keep them from being killed while they're out there, or to analyze the information they send back home. They're the tip of the spear. Rest of us are just plain old wood." She laughs and leads me off toward the central courtyard, which rises up through the plate glass at the top of the stairs. On the walls are flags from Eastern bloc states, pulled down by protesters as they clamored for freedom. Down one hallway, a car sits behind a rope, cut in half to show the hidden compartment officers used to smuggle refugees across the Berlin Wall.

My black-folder envy melts as we walk the echoing halls, past photographs of war and peace and history itself. Every hundred feet or so, we pass a big metal door with a combination lock in place of a handle. Eventually, we stop in front of one.

"Well, Miss New Girl, here we are. Southeast Asia Division. Your branch chief'll take it from here." She opens the door to a giant room-sized safe, filled with desks and the tapping of keys. My new boss is waiting, a bearded, gentle, clever-looking man in corduroys and socks. He looks old enough to be nearing retirement. He explains that we are standing in something called a SCIF, a sensitive compartmented information facility, and that no classified material can be taken out the door without advance clearance.

"That includes the cafeteria," he says.

"Remember, just because everyone else has clearance, they don't get to see what you got and you don't get to see what they got. If you're eating in the cafeteria, your lunch conversation better be about your love life. And none of us has time for one of those. So you might as well just eat here."

I've been assigned to cover Jemaah Islamiyah, the al Qa'ida affiliate in Southeast Asia, reading hundreds of classified cables a day from foreign governments, U.S. diplomats, and our own covert operatives in the field, then synthesizing the intelligence into actionable briefs for congress and the president. It's analytical; it's difficult; and I love it. The hours don't allow for much of a life, though. The president's briefer leaves Langley for the White House every morning before dawn, so I drive my choking old Jeep across the Key Bridge in the dark to brief the briefer on Southeast Asia threats at three-thirty a.m. Then I walk outside to watch the sun rise before the heat of the day sets in.

I'm juggling work with full-time graduate school across the Potomac at Georgetown. I stay in the campus library late and get to my desk at Langley early, making up for the lack of sleep with stale cafeteria coffee. Fatigue becomes a badge of honor. Half-open toiletries kits and makeshift overnight cots abound. My boss has a Lufthansa sticker on his office door that says "Wake for meals."

I fall hard and fast into the world of the Agency. We speak in cryptonyms—"crypts"— and three-letter acronyms. We feel the weight of the world on our shoulders. We get called in at all hours to deal with this crisis or that one. It's as though anything that happens anywhere on the planet is happening to us. As though our every move is important. As though we are important. And it's addictive.

Southeast Asia threats hit especially close to home. Jim and I walked the island of Bali in the aftermath of the 2002 bombings, heard shopkeepers describe the limbs strewn outside their stores. At the time, all I could do was wonder if that was how Laura's limbs had looked, when they hit the ground in Scotland. Now I can work to stop the next attack. Now, a year later, I sit down every morning, enter the numeric code from the digital fob around my neck, and open a list of cables, each of them detailing some new plot. One by one, I scan them and sort them by urgency, aware of what a lapse in concentration might cost. Overlook a credible threat and more limbs end up on the sidewalk. Shut one down too early and lose the chance to arrest the leaders. Harm an innocent bystander and become no better than the men we hunt. It's exhausting and exhilarating, a daily mix of adrenaline and caffeine that lands screeching at the nine a.m. all-hands meeting, where we highlight the most imminent threats for the Clandestine Service to stop before they gather too much steam.

The black-folder, tip-of-the-spear gang doesn't come to the meeting themselves. They send representatives I think of as gray folders—spook look, spook jargon, but stuck here at HQS when they'd rather be out in the field. Some of them tried and didn't make the cut. Others are still training. The worst are the has-beens: former field officers cooling their heels back here at Langley while they do penance or dry out. Like B-list movie stars, they have more attitude than the real-deal operatives. There is an erratic energy about them. They are people with something to prove.

In a nondescript conference room, we take turns outlining the shrillest threats from the morning's cable traffic. For each potential attack, we list what more we need to know before we can write a complete assessment for the president. The gray folders scribble notes to turn into taskings for their field operatives once they get back to their desks. As if by magic, the answers to those questions sit waiting in our queue of cables the following day.

I have some sense of how the questions become answers: field operatives reach out to clandestine sources, moles within terror organizations or foreign governments, and ask them for clarification during late-night car meetings or walks down back lanes. But the Ian Fleming drama of it all seems far removed from the analysis cycle we run through in our Langley cubicles. Here, the focus is on pulling the threads from those different sources together and answering enough of the who, what, where, when, and how for the president to authorize the forces he needs in order to prevent an impending attack.

In the case of Southeast Asia, the biggest threats come from Jemaah Islamiyah, the al Qa'ida offshoot whose leader, a man known as Hambali, has claimed responsibility for the Bali bombings and is an old pal of 9/11 mastermind Khalid Sheikh Mohammed (known in Agency parlance as "KSM"). That link to KSM shoots Jemaah Islamiyah to the top of U.S. concerns, for reasons even more deeply rooted than the destruction of the World Trade Center. KSM's nephew, Ramzi Yousef, is currently cooling his heels at ADX Florence—America's most secure prison—for executing the 1993 World Trade Center bombing. He was caught after fleeing to the Philippines, but not before planning a subsequent attack in which eleven airliners would simultaneously be hijacked, with one plowing into a skyscraper in Manila, killing the pope during his visit from Rome, and another crashing into our very own headquarters building here in Langley, Virginia.

The plot was foiled after Yousef's apartment caught fire and emergency workers discovered his plans, but the possibility of using commercial airliners as missiles had been lodged in his uncle KSM's brain. That idea led to the deaths of 2,996 people on 9/11, and possibly, one more a few months after that. The veins and freckles on the hand that sawed Danny's head from his body turn out to match KSM's.

Day by day, those three letters become a personification of the evil we fight. And KSM's involvement with Jemaah Islamiyah makes this desk the only place in the world where I want to work. I begin to feel as if the reckoning for Danny, and for Laura and those lost on 9/11, too, somehow, comes down to me—to how carefully I read the incoming cables and whether the follow-up questions I ask uncover some detail that can help prevent another explosion, another beheading, another Tuesday morning in lower Manhattan covered with human ash.

When the field operatives can't find answers to my questions, I stare at their cables, my fingers limp on the keys. In those moments, I am powerless, able only to identify threats and the data we need to stop them but incapable of getting on a plane to find the answers myself. I wonder whether this is how some other analyst felt, years earlier, when murmurs of 9/11 rumbled but concrete answers never came. Will I, too, turn on the news to find one of these phantom plots played out in high definition? Will I also know the ache of wondering whether I did enough, here in the sanitized safety of northern Virginia, to counter the threats that bubble daily in my queue?

I graduate from Georgetown in the humidity of the gymnasium as spring rain pounds the windows and soaks the empty chairs arranged around the flagpole. I've managed to get out of here with honors. But I don't really know the place, I realize, as I scan the pendants and statues that line the walls. I ducked in and out and submitted my papers, but I never stopped processing whatever cable or threat report I had just read long enough to feel that I belonged here, amid the removed academia of the Bulldogs' blue and gray. I look at the other students who studied alongside me, wonder how many of them are going on to the same career, in some different SCIF in some different unmarked building. Wonder how many of us have felt at home here, or will feel at home anywhere again.

A few weeks after graduation, my boss hands me a letter. He looks at me with a mix of paternal pride and sadness. "Clandestine Service wants you." The black folders flash in my mind's eye. "Bastards were just waiting for you to finish school." The adrenaline hits me hard as he talks. It's the scariest invitation I've ever been given and the one invitation I've most wanted to receive. I got into this business to understand the people who attacked us, so I could make them stop. With this single letter, I might finally have the chance to meet them face-to-face.

It's bittersweet, leaving the analysts' world of synthesis and briefings. I'm trading in my bird's-eye view for a glimpse of the truth on the ground. I won't see the whole picture anymore, won't understand the way the pieces fit together at the top. But at least now I'll get to try answering the questions myself. No more sending queries out into the ether, hoping blindly that the data we need to stop an attack turns up on my screen in the morning.

—

I show up the following week, as the letter instructs, at the main headquarters auditorium, a quirky midcentury dome affectionately known as the Bubble. On a table at the back of the vestibule is a pile of black folders.

"Agency identification number?" the security officer asks. I reel off the seven digits and he riffles through the pile, then hands me a folder. "Welcome to the Clandestine Service, Ms. Tanner," he says, and I fight the urge to look behind myself for the woman he's talking to. It's a training name, used to ensure that even our own classmates don't know our true identities—an added measure of protection, in case one of us finds ourselves under duress in the field. We'll be trained to withstand captivity and torture, but not knowing the information we're being asked to reveal is the greatest protection of all.

I press through the swinging doors, into the auditorium. Only the first few rows are occupied—by no more than fifty others, with their black folders in their laps.

"Good morning, Class 17," a man says from the stage. It seems impossible that there could be so few of us. "You've probably heard that you're this country's best and her brightest. Well, I won't comment on that except to say, Don't expect to be treated with kid gloves. We are facing a multiheaded monster out there, and the nation has never been more in need of your service. It's not going to be easy, but we plan to prevail. So I hope you're ready to get to work."

A few recruits let out a whoop or a Marine Corps grunt. Most sit rapt but silent. One or two fidget with their folders. I scan the row to either side of me. Trainees have to be under the age of thirty-five, but other than that general youth, there's no unifying feature. More men than women, more white than non, but not by much. Some drape an arm over their chair with prep school cool. Some wear worn shoes and mended clothes. There are jocks and dorks, poets and mathematicians. I wonder how each of them got to this moment. Somehow, in the strangeness, there is kinship. And I feel oddly at home in their midst.

The man continues, standing between an American flag and a CIA seal. The

Clandestine Service puts its recruits through a year-long training course in field tradecraft, he tells us, much of which is undertaken at a remote military base known as the Farm. But first we're to do a stint at headquarters, learning the ropes of the operations desks and giving the powers that be a chance to assess us in the wild. He tells us to check our folders for our assignments.

My breath catches for a beat as I thumb past a page of passcodes to find out where I'll be spending the next six months. When my eyes fall on the words, I exhale hard. The Iraq desk in the Counterterrorism Center. It's the center of the fight, just as al Qa'ida in Iraq leader Abu Musab al-Zarqawi is starting to take his stranglehold on Baghdad and Anbar.

"Good news?" the man sitting beside me asks.

"To the extent that car bombs and air strikes can be considered good news, sure," I say, and he smiles.

"At least you're in the middle of shit. I got West Africa."

It's a strange gauge we all use, proximity to death. But in it, we find proximity to the chance that death might be averted. And by that strange, double-edged measure, CTC/Iraq is choice meat.

It's emotionally grueling work. My first

task is to watch the same beheading video a hundred times in a row, focusing on a different grid square of the image each time to note any overlooked clue it might give to the location of the crime.

I wade through hundreds of hours of debriefing videos. I build room-sized maps of phone connections between Zarqawi's lieutenants. I come to know them better than I know most of my friends—to understand what still haunts them about their childhood, how a particular string of numbers holds emotional significance for them, the different reasons each gets up every day to fight.

Throughout the week, we get pulled out for briefings, alongside the other Clandestine Service trainees, a reinforcing of our group dynamic, a setting apart of our little band from the giant spaceship of people who will support us when we deploy. Between meet-ups, we e-mail one another jokes and gossip and suggestions for weekend plans. We rendezvous for lunch or to run administrative errands in the labyrinth of the headquarters basement.

There is a stand-alone window in one of the hallway walls down there, deep in the heart of the maze, behind which an old, cranky, begrudgingly beloved secretary named Ruth generates code names for new operations. We've learned to tromp down there, rattling freshly approved forms, golden tickets to embark on new, as-yet-unnamed missions. Into Ruth's hands they go, and down comes the window shutter; a moment later, it flies up again and she hands us, with a sly smile, the name by which our next op will be known. In theory, the names are generated at random. But as every trainee soon learns, they bear an uncanny relationship to just how much Ruth likes you.

"Guess we shouldn'ta kept her into her lunch break," my friend says one day, and he holds up a card with OPERATION INCESSANT HUNGER typed in all caps.

We stop at the hot dog machine on our way back upstairs. As far as anyone can tell, the hot dog machine has existed in the basement of CIA headquarters since dinosaurs roamed the earth. Nobody knows who put it there. And nobody has ever seen it being restocked. Yet there it sits, at the crossroads of two undecorated hallways, deep underground, spitting out sizzling hot dogs for generations of bleary-eyed spies.

"Kind of reminds me of the Zoltar machine in **Big**," I say as it bangs and chugs its way to producing my lunch.

"Well, here's our fortune," my friend jokes, and he flips a playing card out of his pocket and onto the glass. It's from one of the decks the Counterterrorism Center has issued its officers to keep track of its highest-priority targets—one card per terrorist it's tasked to kill.

"Haji al-Yemeni?" I ask.

He nods. "Bad dude," he says. "Chief assigned him to us. Last seen in Algeria." The hot dog machine lurches with the final efforts of its labor.

"You know that's not a real name," I say, watching the machine ooze on the relish. "It's an honorific, like saying 'Mr. Doctor.' It just means someone who's completed the hajj who comes from Yemen. And most Yemenis are Muslims, and all Muslims are supposed to complete the hajj. So Haji al-Yemeni isn't one person—it's basically half the population of an entire country."

The machine dings and presents my hot dog with exhausted glee.

"Yeah, well, it's on a baseball card," he says, and hands me the laminated rectangle.

Back upstairs, I look up the name in our central computer system. He's not wrong. There's a huge file.

Agency cables are almost as anachronistic

as the hot dog machine. Typed in all caps, using the same indecipherable routing markers they required back in the punch-card, predigital days, thousands of them arrive at Langley every day, covering everything from administrative expense reports to highly classified intelligence about pending attacks. Among the cryptic symbols hidden within the actual text is a pair of double brackets placed around a person's surname—a signal to the system that it should log a copy of the cable in that person's file. Which means that a cable from any CIA station, anywhere in the world, containing the name HAJI [[AL-YEMENI]], will be copied to a single bulging master file. And, man, has the system been busy.

There are over a hundred separate pieces of intelligence describing plots this phantom name is planning. They come from almost a dozen countries in three different continents, none of which is Arabic-speaking. In the frenzy to count scalps in the Global War on Terror, stations from Reykjavik to Rio have been submitting threat reports from local assets, who themselves have learned that terror tips pay handsomely, whether verified or not. And it turns out that when neither assets nor operatives speak Arabic, the threat reports about generic Mr. Doctors begin to add up fast.

I flag my chief down as she passes my cubicle on her way back from the seventh floor, where members of the senior leadership have their offices.

"Are there any safeguards to stop this from happening?"

She shakes her head. "These guys use so many names," she says, as if she's describing the biological advantages of an alien, off-world enemy.

"No," I say. "I mean, yes, they do. But this is different. This is our error. It's like making a list of all the crimes committed by Americans who have a bachelor's degree and then using it to arrest any American who has a bachelor's degree."

"Nobody said it would be easy," she says, and nods, like now maybe I understand the magnitude of our burden.

"No, sorry," I press on. "I mean, I'm not pointing out that it's hard. I'm pointing out that we're doing it wrong. Innocent people are going to get killed."

She jerks her head at the poster of the twin towers on the wall and says curtly, "They already have."

I sit there dizzy for a minute, as though

I've been blindfolded and spun around a few times. Innocent people died. That's why we're all here, in this building of beige, room-sized safes, trying to stop it from happening again. How does that make it logical to kill every Yemeni who has completed the hajj? On a practical level, killing innocents ties up resources and makes future enemies. On a moral level, it leaves us nothing worth fighting for.

I start searching out other common honorifics, working off my meager grad school Arabic. I find a cable from an Afghan black site—a secret prison—code-named Salt Pit. They had a man named Khaled al-Masri in custody, it says. The cable doesn't mention that al-Masri means someone who comes from Egypt. Or that Khaled is the third most common Egyptian name. Or that there are literally over a million Khaled al-Masris in the world. It says simply that Khaled al-Masri was rendered from Macedonia, when his name was found on the list of high-value targets. It goes on to say that the Salt Pit leadership was later satisfied that they had rendered the wrong person and planned to reverse the rendition, releasing Khaled al-Masri with no public admission of error.

It is not until years later that I learn the

full human truth behind that cable. Reading the results of a FISA (Foreign Intelligence Surveillance Act) request in the open press, I learn that al-Masri had been on his way home to his wife and two kids when local police officers noticed that his name matched one on the American watch list. Holiday season as it was, the officers were hungrier than usual for American reward money. They locked him in a motel room and called the CIA station in Skopje. The deputy chief coordinated with the Counterterrorism Center back at Langley and, based on nothing more than that honorific, they sent over a team of men dressed in black, their faces covered by masks. The men held Khaled down as he frantically asked who they were, called out for his wife. They didn't answer him. Just silently cut off his clothes, fit him with a diaper, a jumpsuit, and a blindfold. Injected him with sedative. And flew him to Afghanistan.

When he woke, he was told he was beyond the law. He was beaten, electrocuted, starved. Every week, a man he took to be a doctor came in to sample his blood and urine. Throughout it all, he maintained his innocence. Eventually, he resorted to a hunger strike. They held him down and stuck a feeding tube up his nose.

Four months later, someone down the hall from his bound and force-fed body wrote that sterile cable I read on my screen in Virginia: WE ARE SATISFIED WE HAVE RENDERED THE WRONG MAN.

They dropped him on a dirt road in Albania, instructing him not to look back. He suffered permanent spinal damage. He had lost sixty pounds. His wife thought he had left her and had divorced him. He shook whenever the overhead lights started to hum.

And nobody ever told him they were sorry.

Long before knowing all that, still a trainee with a hot dog on my desk, I stare at the Salt Pit cable on my screen. Stare at the name, KHALED [[AL-MASRI]], double-bracketed in all caps, full of the brazen confidence of the overzealous and underinformed.

"We've got an honorifics problem," I tell my branch chief.

"Not this again." She bats a hand, waving me away, without glancing up from her computer.

"It's not just al-Yemeni. The same thing happened with Khaled al-Masri." She recognizes the name but doesn't stop typing. I continue: "There're another twenty, maybe thirty, from what I can tell. And that's just the ones we've acted on. And just the ones I'm cleared to see."

"Okay," she says, eyes still glued to her screen. "You're authorized to fix it."

I'm at a loss for what to say. I'm a first-year trainee. How am I supposed to fix it?

For a second, there's just the clicking of her fingers on the keys.

"Fine," I reply, "but you need to stop the renditions until I do."

Now she looks at me. "Are you out of your goddamned mind?"

"We're kidnapping random, innocent people—"

She interrupts me: "You want to answer to Congress, kid? Come another 9/11, I'd rather say we rendered a hundred innocent assholes than tell them we let one fucking terrorist go free."

"I think you have it backward," I mumble.

"What?"

"The quote. It's Benjamin Franklin. 'Better one hundred guilty persons should escape than one innocent person should suffer.'"

She locks eyes with me and says, "He was talking about Americans."

9

I take my first trip to meet a detainee in person. I arrive wearing a hijab. He arrives wearing a hood. He gets to take his off. I don't. We talk about Kafka. He's surprised when I quote from the Qur'an. I'm surprised when he quotes Malcolm X.

I ask if he has a window in his cell. He says he does—a little one, though at night, he can see Orion's Belt. He says he likes that cluster of stars because it reminds him that humans see the same truth but call it by different words. In the West, we call those balls of fire Orion's Belt, to honor a heroic hunter. In Arabic, the same stars are called the String of Pearls, to honor the wisdom that grows from suffering. It's not what I expected to hear from underneath that hood, when Mahmoud first shuffled into that room.

By the time I leave, we're still military adversaries, but we're also something like friends. He tells me what he knows about the back room of a furniture store, where men are stashing explosives for a Frankentruck—the Agency's colloquial term for a truck-borne explosive device, with a suicide bomber at the wheel and sometimes another man on the roof. He doesn't agree with the target. Too many civilians. It isn't waterboarding or enhanced interrogation that uncovers the location of those lethal heaps of nails and explosives. It's slow, hard-won mutual respect. And another few Tetris tiles of understanding fall into place.

—

As I spend more and more of my hours at Langley, I have less and less time to spend on the phone with Anthony, a problem to which the solution should be breaking up. Instead, he tells me he wants to move to the United States. To Virginia. To my cramped one-bedroom, with its sink full of cereal bowls.

He's a foreign national and I'm not cleared to so much as kiss a foreign national, let alone live with one. The only way around this restriction is to get engaged, at which point the review board would be allowed to grant an exception. But Anthony doesn't know where I work, so explaining this need to get married is tough. I suggest that we tie the knot to qualify him for a longer visa. He laughs. "Getting sentimental, huh, Indy?" he asks. It's a reference to Indiana Jones, and no, I'm not getting sentimental. In fact, I'm increasingly dreading his arrival. But at each fork in the road, I dread the drama of breaking up just a little bit more. And so he boards a flight to Dulles.

I go and stand there in the greeters' spot and wait for him, surrounded by people with balloons. He comes through the door, smelling like two years haven't passed.

"How was your flight?" I ask.

"You cut your hair," he says, and takes the ends in his fingers.

Outside, a supersized American flag waves above the cars glinting in the parking lot. He talks as we walk, filling my silence with stories of people we once knew. All I can focus on is what's about to happen. It's an insanely unfair thing to do to someone you love.

"I can't wait to get home," he says, and we climb into my Jeep, as though home is where we are going.

Instead, I drive us to a building in

Arlington, where a man dressed as a garage attendant checks my ID.

"Second floor. Leave your phones in the car," he says.

Anthony watches me roll up the window.

"This is gonna be weird," I tell him, "but just be yourself and we can go."

"Are we auditioning for a reality show?" he jokes. I'd forgotten that he jokes when he's nervous.

"Kinda," I say, and put my phone in the glove box.

Inside, the wall beside the elevator is lined with names and suite numbers. Dentists and accountants. I'm not sure if they're real or put there for show. If they're real, they don't know what goes on in Suite 201. Anthony takes my hand.

I wonder, as the sliding doors close and reopen, whether I'm doing this because I want to be with him. Or whether I'm doing it because I don't want to break up with him. And whether those two things are the same.

"Remove all jewelry" reads a sign propped up on the waiting room table, amid worn copies of **The Economist**. There is no receptionist. I notice a camera in the corner, above the clock.

When the inner door finally opens, the

man on the other side reads out a string of digits.

I nod. It's my Agency identification number, used to avoid revealing real-world identities anytime we can.

"This way." He waves us into a beige hallway with geometric prints and looped nylon carpet. The walls are lined with doors.

He overtakes us and punches a code into a keypad beside one of the door frames. The door opens to a small office. Against one wall is a desk. Against another is a chair. Around the chair, like a halo, is a tangle of wires. Some connect to dials, others to elastics and hooks and belts. On one side, a padded platform stands ready to support a strapped-in forearm.

"That's a lie-detector machine," Anthony says. "I've seen them on **Jerry Springer**." He laughs. The man doesn't. "Is it true," Anthony asks, "you can beat these things by tightening your sphincter?" He's really nervous now. The tips of his ears are pink. I want to hug him, but I'm worried that the man will think I'm whispering secret instructions.

"Just be yourself," I say again, and the man leads me back out into the hallway, into an adjacent room with a window in its wall. I can see Anthony, in his docksiders and teddy bear socks, sitting in the chair, surrounded by the wires. He's looking at a potted flower on the desk.

"Be kind to him," I say.

"Just doing my job, ma'am," the man says back. And then he is in the room again, and I watch him hook the wires across Anthony's chest.

He sits on the edge of the desk.

"Can you tell me what day of the week it is," he begins.

"Look, what's going on," Anthony asks.

"I'll explain in a minute. If you could just answer the question, sir."

There's a long pause.

"Sunday," Anthony says.

"Thank you. And what state are we in?"

"Virginia, I think."

"Thank you. Have you ever lied on your taxes?"

The man's voice has no inflections. Anthony's eyes flick to the mirror. At least he knows I'm here. At least he knows he's not alone.

"What is this?" he asks again.

"Really, sir, it would go so much quicker."

"Probably, okay, yes, I've probably fudged my taxes at some stage. My British taxes, I might add. But out of confusion, okay? Not malice. I'm not an accountant."

He's doing great. The less professional he seems at this, the better. Flustered is fine. Flaky is fine. Even tax fraud is fine. Just so long as no one thinks he's a spy.

The man asks a few more baseline questions in his emotionless drone voice. Then he pulls a long piece of paper out of a printer embedded in the desk and studies the squiggly lines. It's not clear to me if they actually mean anything or if the whole kit and caboodle is a giant prop in a game of psychological warfare. I'm not sure it's even clear to the man.

"Look, am I required to be here?" Anthony asks.

"No. You can leave at any time. But if you leave, you won't be able to see your fiancée again."

For the first time, a look of genuine fear passes across Anthony's face, and I know it's occurring to him I am in danger. The man sees it, too.

"She's fine. We just need to be certain you don't pose her—or us—any threat."

Anthony looks unsure whether to laugh or run.

"Amaryllis is employed by the United States Central Intelligence Agency," the man explains. "Did you know that?"

Anthony stares at him, looks to the mirror, turns back to the man, shakes his head.

"I need a verbal response," the man says.

"No," Anthony answers.

"I need a complete sentence," the man says.

Anthony stares at him a beat longer. "No, I did not know that Amaryllis is employed by the United States Central Intelligence Agency." His tone is hollow, as if his innards have been kicked out. The man marks inflection points on the printer paper with a felt-tipped pen. Then Anthony's voice again, softer: "But I believe she has a good reason if she is."

Suddenly, I am crying.

"Do you currently or have you ever worked for any intelligence organization?"

"Do you now or have you ever held any affiliation with a violent resistance movement?"

On and on the man drones.

"Are you now or have you ever been a member of the Communist Party?"

Anthony laughs.

"You guys know its 2003, right?"

When the exam is over and the man opens the door, I stand there in the nylon-carpeted hallway, bracing for Anthony's anger. For a second, his face is blank. Then he cracks a grin.

"Aw, come on. You didn't think a little thing like a secret identity would scare me off, did you, Indy?"

It's like being accepted by some ancient part of myself. He's the first person from my old world, my real world, to know my truth. And he loves me anyway. It's almost enough to make me feel whole. And so I ignore the tugging fractures between what was and what is. I drive him home and unpack his bags.

—

The Agency wastes no time before it starts breathing down our necks, urging us to make good on our promise. We either get married or risk losing the provisional permit to sleep in the same bed. A city hall wedding would confuse my family and raise too many questions. After all, getting engaged at twenty-three is really only believable if you come across as a serious romantic. That, and Anthony has always wanted a big cathedral wedding. Given what I've put him through, it seems like I owe him that much. So it's real-deal pomp and circumstance or bust.

I'm working Baghdad kidnapping cases, matching audio samples from beheading videos with street noise from locations where we think American prisoners might be detained. Planning a wedding is the last thing on my mind. But each week I get an increasingly breathless note from the security office, checking on my marriage status as though it's a matter of national security. Eventually, I call my mom and set about choosing fabric swatches.

She probes gently as we pick china patterns and examine reception brochures. Am I sure? Aren't I a bit young? Couldn't we give it a little more time? I want to tell her that I've already signed my life away. I want to tell her that I'm just trying to do what my country is asking of me. I want to tell her that I don't feel like I have a choice. Instead I say, "When you know, you know."

In the evenings, I forgo drinks with my Agency brothers to play board games with Anthony at our local pub. Scrabble and Trivial Pursuit and Risk. We eat French fries and don't talk about work. There is a salve to it, like the silence between sets of intense music. Some nights, it even feels like enough.

We get married in the Washington National Cathedral on a bright April afternoon. The building is echoey and vast, but to me it is the most intimate of hiding places, the scene of my high school daydreams and secret, stolen lunchtimes. In its pews and corners, I read **Catcher in the Rye, Crime and Punishment,**

Siddhartha, Of Mice and Men. In its subterranean chapels, I talked to the universe and to Laura and to God. And so I feel safe here, cradled in the arms of an ancient stony friend, as the first bars of "Ave Maria" begin to play and my sisters glide ahead of me down the vaulted aisle.

I walk toward the altar, past work friends whose real names I'll never know. Above me, a piece of moon rock hangs suspended in a stained-glass window. I think of my mother reading me **The Little Prince**, remember the man in that book, counting all the stars he owns without realizing he owns nothing at all. You don't own a piece of the universe just because you say so, my mother had explained. Someone should tell that to al Qa'ida in Iraq, I think. And to our generals, too, while they're at it.

Anthony watches me walk toward him, a knowing look on his face. I can no more give myself to him than I can spend the money I've already paid in taxes. The government has taken more than its tithe. The coffers are bare. But he loves me for making the effort, and I love him for letting me try.

Afterward, an evening rain sweeps in. We jump out of the car on the way home from the reception and share a smoke under the pitter-patter of rain on our umbrella, sitting side by side in our wedding clothes on the steps of the Lincoln Memorial.

"Bosses'll be happy now?" he asks.

"I'm not sure happy's in their vocabulary," I say as the rain falls around us like a curtain. "But I am."

And in that moment, it's true.

—

The next month, I get assigned to CTC/WMD, the portion of the Counterterrorism Center responsible for keeping nuclear, biological, and chemical weapons out of the hands of terrorists. We don't focus on state programs like Iran's or North Korea's. Our purview is strictly nonstate actors—mostly al Qa'ida and its affiliates, but also the smugglers that supply them.

Traditional targets, like the officials who run the Iranian or North Korean programs, can be approached by CIA officers posing as State Department diplomats. But our targets— arms dealers and their terrorist clients—are just as unlikely to talk with a State Department employee as with an officer from CIA. To them, we're all U.S. government lackeys, and they avoid the U.S. government—avoid all governments—like the plague.

To get near our type of targets, the Agency uses a different approach. Instead of playing diplomats, officers under nonofficial cover, known as NOCs, pose as businesspeople or aid workers—anything that gives them access to the world of their targets, while avoiding the stench of officialdom.

Not only are the field operatives under nonofficial cover, but their commanding base is as well. It's too risky for a NOC to report to Langley when they visit D.C. That right turn off Route 123 could burn hundreds of thousands of dollars in elaborate cover if the wrong person should happen to see. And so their operations are run out of nondescript office suites, high up in nondescript office buildings, deep in the sprawl of northern Virginia.

It's my first time working in a safe house under commercial cover. It's my first time working in an office building at all. And I savor the banal normalcy of it. The Ruby Tuesday in the lobby. The chitchat of paralegals blotting their lipstick in the bathroom. They have no idea that in their midst we track missing suitcase nukes and intercept strains of smallpox and anthrax. But they play their role. Their faces flash in my mind every time we add a casualty estimate to a given threat report. They are the humans we are protecting, in all their beautiful, everyday glory.

Behind the double set of doors on the twenty-second floor, we write dozens of those threat reports. Run nightmarish simulations based on plots we intercept on the terror cell wires. The hardest part is conveying the sheer scale to policy makers in terms they can understand. The population of lower Manhattan, every kid in the U.S. public school system, the entire U.S. water supply.

One report talks about a martyrdom operation where instead of blowing himself up, the bomber would infect himself with a lethal virus and sit on the New York City subway system, breathing, until he dies. We run the simulation. It takes under two weeks to reach urban breakdown point—the death of 10 percent of the city's population. One attacker, hundreds of thousands of casualties.

"Guess that's why they call it asymmetrical warfare," I say to my deskmate.

"What did they call Hiroshima?" he asks.

10

I feed on the frenetic pace, justify my growing distance from Anthony by repeating like a mantra the importance of my work. In the echo chamber of my Agency brothers, it's easy. Sipping burnt coffee before dawn or rail tequila after midnight, we judge ourselves— and one another—by the scale of catastrophe we're averting. "You know the problem with that?" Anthony asks me one night as we weave our way home from an Irish pub crawl with the crew. "You guys have to keep making up apocalypses so you can keep finding self-worth in preventing them."

It's an uncomfortably simple piece of logic. But I picture the pile of red-bordered cables on my desk and say, "Luckily for us, al Qa'ida's already made up a couple hundred apocalypses to work through before we'll have to go making up any of our own."

Getting married for administrative reasons at twenty-four turns out not to be the best idea, especially a month before moving into the most elite operational training program on earth. I start the CIA Field Tradecraft course in the fall, learning the basics of elicitation, dead drops, bumps, brush passes, and surveillance detection; afterward, some of us will be chosen to undergo further operational training at the rambling covert base in Virginia known as the Farm.

My small band of classmates and I run around D.C. at all hours of the day and night, marking signal sites with chalk and identifying the license plates of the cars that trail us, sorting the training surveillants from the real ones, high on the fact that the civilians around us are carrying on with their normal days, oblivious to what is happening right in front of them.

We're given our first operational assessment: a bump, which means finding a target of interest in some public place and manufacturing a reason to get them talking. The aim is the much-coveted "second meeting": an opportunity to continue the conversation somewhere else at some later date; this offers the operative the chance to build a relationship and, with it, access to whatever information the target might hold. I know from my time at CTC how precious that information can be. The location of a detainee, delivered hours before she's to be beheaded. The name of a seller on his way to provide Soviet-era tactical nukes to a contact in al Qa'ida. The security loophole Hizb'allah plans to exploit to walk catastrophic biological agents out of a scientist's deep freezer.

The targets we're given during training are all characters played by case officers, the real-life, battle-hardened spies we trainees aspire someday to be. Some play the roles out of a sense of duty, passing their skills on to the next generation. Others do it out of exhaustion, craving a plum three-year tour back home. The rest do it by way of penalty box, paying their dues after screwing up—or screwing someone—somewhere out there at the tip of the spear.

Our instructor drops folders on the tables in front of us, one each, all black. Mine opens with a photo of a middle-aged Gorbachev look-alike, minus the port-wine stain, leaning against the bar in a crowded pub. The write-up is sparse. He's a Kazakh civil servant, it says. He knows about an imminent attack to be carried out with his government's blessing. He has objected—privately, of course.

He was ignored. The local station believes he might be a viable target. Beyond that, there are only a few words of bio. He went to the Kazakh-American University in Almaty and studied business, with a minor in film. He collects American baseball cards. He has a dog. Tacked onto the end is a surveillance report. His home, the ministry, the home of his lover. Sometimes, on Sundays, he likes to go to Panera Bread. I smile at the awkward allowance for a location near the training center. Guess that's where I'm headed. My eye scans the rest of the page. He sits in the back, it says. He always orders the pie.

I pull into a spot in the suburban Panera parking lot. I'm driving a training car, a rented Dodge Stratus, designed to safeguard my cover from any real-world surveillants sent by the Russians or Chinese to get a jump on identifying the CIA's next cohort of spies. Fair enough—my rust-bucket Jeep is pretty identifiable. I glance in the rearview mirror. This is going to be our first graded exercise. My reflection doesn't inspire confidence. **Blotchy skin, nervous eyes, the puppy chub of childhood still in her cheeks.** Every movie I've ever watched suggests this is not what spies look like. But then, I guess spies who look like spies don't get very far.

Inside Panera, a line of Sunday brunchers snakes toward the door. I scan the room over the top of a menu, feeling vaguely ridiculous. The weekend yuppie crowd sprawls across tables and chairs. No sign of a cranky case officer posing as a Kazakh informant, pretending not to know I'm there. For a minute I wonder if I've dreamed the whole thing, the way crazy people always think they're surrounded by the CIA. And then I see him. Sitting in the back at the coffee bar, shoulders hunched, as if he's nursing a finger of whiskey.

This is it. My first opportunity to mess something up so badly I get kicked out of the program. I draw breath and head toward him. The stool next to him is free—a courtesy for a new student, I'm pretty sure. I sit down and set a laptop and a book on the bar. He's waiting for me to make the first move. I let him wait. In part because I'm terrified. And in part because I think it seems more natural that way. I open my laptop to an e-mail template and begin typing a fake note. "Thanks for the heads-up," I tap to a fictional correspondent. "Given my connections in Washington, I feel a responsibility to help—I'm sure you understand." I leave the cursor blinking there for a minute. I can feel him stealing a glance at my screen. I force myself not to look for his look.

Instead, I sigh. Wait a beat longer. Then hit the keystroke combo to lock the screen.

"Do you mind?" I ask him. He looks startled. "Watching my things," I say. "Would you mind keeping an eye on them while I use the restroom?" He glances at the laptop, the book, back to me. He nods. The book is a prop I've created by wrapping a novel in a handmade cover that reads: **Rat Pack Chic: Glamour, Freedom, and the Advent of American Cool.**

In the bathroom, I pull the door shut and start counting: **One, two, three.** I look in the mirror, examine my reflection again: **Fourteen, fifteen, sixteen.** She looks better this time. **Twenty-two, twenty-three, twenty-four.** Like maybe she just might make it through this thing alive. **Twenty-eight, twenty-nine, thirty.** I open the door and clock him right where I left him, eyeing the picture of Dean Martin and Sinatra in mid-croon.

"Thanks," I say and sit back down. We fall silent for a beat. It's unbearable, the waiting. Then finally, he says, "Those were the days, huh?" and nods toward the photo on the book's cover like a spurned lover gesturing toward the girl who passed him by.

"Weren't they, though," I say. "I've always

kind of wished I were born back then. I collect their letters." I give him a shy smile. "The Rat Pack. You know, I mean I buy their letters and things when I get the chance."

His face brightens. "I'd love to see those sometime." He's making this easy.

"Well, I've been planning to digitize them, you know, make them available online. Seems like such a waste for them to be in my desk drawer. But I haven't gotten around to it yet."

"That's too bad," he says, and I can hear the opening in his voice.

"But, you know, I'd be happy to give you a look. You've been so kind, watching my things and everything. And I love meeting other people who appreciate the good old times. When things were . . ." I pause. Glance at the television screen in the corner. "Simpler."

"There, I also know what you mean," he says as the news anchor turns to talk of terrorism. "I'd be happy to have an hour's escape in the company of Frank Sinatra."

I smile. "It's a deal, then. How can I reach you?"

He begins to give me his phone number, then stops and stares at me for a second.

"Helluva first meeting, kid." He's broken character. This is how the exercise ends, I guess. The Kazakh evaporates and only the case officer remains, with the Brooklyn still in him. "Nice approach, asking me a favor. Most of your idiot comrades just sidle up and blurt out some awkward conversation starter like they have geopolitical Tourette's. Why the Rat Pack?"

"You . . . he . . . collects old U.S. baseball cards. I figured having some of those was a bit too on the nose. But, y'know, Joe DiMaggio, Marilyn Monroe, Sinatra—it felt like the same vibe somehow. Servicing some sense of nostalgia. Some yearning for a world that he worries has disappeared."

The guy's laughing at me now. "Regular Dr. Freud," he says with a shake of his head. "But you're right. A good case officer is as much psychology student as he is James Bond."

"Or she," I say.

"Indeed." He pulls an assessment paper out of his back pocket. There are a dozen or so categories students are to be judged on. Beside each, there is a box to check: Satisfactory, Less Than Satisfactory, Unsatisfactory. There is no Good. In this business, it's survive or not. Thrive is not an option. He clicks open his pen and draws a straight line down through the Satisfactory column. At the bottom, in the section for notes, he writes, "All aces. A velvet hammer. Might just have found her calling."

Then he folds the page in quarters, hands it to me, and walks out.

My two closest Agency brothers—Mike and Dave—are waiting for me at Ireland's Four Courts, a mock old country pub along northern Virginia's commuter corridor. They also passed, but each with a smattering of "Less Than Satisfactory"s, or "Lesters," as they are lovingly known. We peruse each other's assessment sheets as we drop shots into our pints of Guinness. "The velvet hammer, eh?" Dave asks. And from then on, that is what he calls me.

As the pace of training quickens, we meet up after every exercise, full of stories and bluster. Anthony joins us sometimes. He adds a certain British humor to our boozy debriefs. Everyone likes him. I like him. But slowly, and then quickly, we are leaving him behind.

He doesn't understand our acronyms, doesn't get the punch lines of our jokes, isn't cleared to know the tradecraft we're learning on the street or the threats we're analyzing back at HQS. He is on the far side of a veil designed to keep outsiders at bay, and I begin to understand why everyone dates inside the Agency. I get home from midnight exercises to find him sitting on our Arlington apartment floor, eyes closed, opera blaring, and a half-empty whiskey bottle beside him. He asks me to get him an interview—believes that if he can just join us. . . . And I try—but it doesn't really work that way.

At the end of the course, my boss calls me into his office. I've been fast-tracked to undergo advanced operations training, despite being a year shy of the formal age threshold of twenty-five. That means six months on a secret base with no communication home. My friends and family will all believe I'm on a consulting gig for the boring multinational. "My advice is to get drunk," my boss tells me, "then get some sleep, then spend some quality time with the people you love. Because in three weeks, you're going to disappear."

I laugh. "For six months or forever?"

He answers with a wry smile. "Depends how literal you are."

—

On a clear, cold winter day, Anthony drives me to a gas station on Route 123 a little before dawn. I kiss him, then leave him standing there, raw and stoic, in the empty gas station forecourt, his hands thrust into his peacoat pockets as he watches me climb into the warm camaraderie of a crowded beige van.

Jokes masking our nerves, we drive through the familiar gates at Langley, pile out of the van and into the blacked-out bus that will deliver us to the Farm—a simulated **Truman Show** set in a fictionalized country called the Republic of Vertania (ROV), where we are to undergo the most demanding espionage training on earth. We are to play the roles of first-tour case officers assigned to the U.S. embassy in the ROV city of Womack. We each have training names—aliases to protect our identities from one another. But other than that, everything feels real. There is an actual embassy building, with an American flag fluttering out front, on an actual town square with a wooden gazebo. There's a cable news channel, like CNN, that reports the news of this fictional universe: Prime Minister Carlin did this or the Sons of Artemis blew up that. There are diplomats visiting from neighboring countries, including a North Korea–style rogue state called the Democratic People's Republic of Vertania (DPRV).

Just like in Panera, every citizen of the ROV, every newscaster, every bombastic DPRV diplomat, every person we interact with in this giant game of make-believe, is played by a CIA operative, assigned to the Farm for a tour as an instructor. And every one of them has a thousand stories—like that time a highly sensitive source brought a six-piece mariachi band to a covert meeting in a back alley at midnight. They have pro tips, too, about things not covered in the training curriculum, like carrying Rolaids to make signal marks on brick because it's less incriminating than chalk, in case of capture and search.

They break character to share these gems with us for only a few hours each night in the sanctity of our SCIFs, the small room-sized safes where five of us work on our cables and intelligence reports under the watchful eye of our advisers. The rest of the time, they stay in character, talking about the impact of the upcoming fake elections on the value of the country's fake currency, speculating about weapons proliferation across the fake border with the DPRV, and worrying about threats from fake terror groups like the ever-more-violent Sons of Artemis.

We go to embassy parties, bump our targets, recruit our assets. We drive off the base in cars tricked out with concealment compartments for our notes and dread unannounced searches at the roadside, our knees in the gravel and our graduation dependent on not having anything incriminating lying about in the cup holders.

The crises ramp up quickly. Soon our every night's sleep is interrupted by urgent walk-ins reporting imminent threats and simulated terror attacks. We're under constant surveillance, pitted against one another, tested well beyond our limits. Sleazy instructors grope the female students in the name of preparing them for harassment in the field. Aging instructors shout at any student who uses the Internet or, God forbid, a cell phone. Division chiefs from Langley go undercover as instructors to identify the best talent in the crop, then secretly undermine their own picks so other chiefs won't notice them.

A multilayered game takes hold. On one level, we recruit the fictional characters played by instructors in the world of the ROV. On a second, we recruit the real-life instructors who will decide who graduates. All the while, we continue to play a third, long-distance level, recruiting chiefs back at HQS to ensure the best real-world assignment if we do make it. All without ever breaking character.

It's exhausting. And like the running millipede, we learn to avoid thinking about how we do it all for fear of tripping up.

Every so often, we are given a free weekend. I don't tell Anthony that. I can't face him. The realness of him. The questions he'll ask and the shedding of so many fictional identities that I'll have to endure to answer them. Instead, I meet up with classmates at random clusters of Holiday Inns and Red Robins. We revel in the anonymity of American suburbia. We see movies in cineplexes. We eat pancakes at Cracker Barrel. And sometimes, most times, we have sex.

—

As the Farm weeks wear on, we take targets through the entire recruitment cycle: spot, assess, develop, recruit, run, terminate. Spotting is spy-speak for noticing people with interesting access at the embassy parties or events around "town"—access that could prevent an attack or give insight into an adversary's plans. Assessment is the dance we go through with HQS to confirm that access, then determine whether the target might be sympathetic to approach and, if so, what kind. Development is where the time and talent come in. Building a relationship with the target over weeks, months, years.

Finding genuine commonality. Nurturing trust. Slowly revealing more and more of the truth about having "special access to Washington." Testing the waters. Until, finally, recruitment—the money shot. At its worst, this is a transactional pitch, buying access to information in exchange for access to something else—medicine, a visa, the cash to clear a debt. At its best, it's one of the most soulful, vulnerable moments two humans can share. A leap of faith to make the world a little safer, while putting their lives, their families' lives, in each other's care. Those are the relationships that last decades, that end wars, that prevent attacks. Those are the relationships that change history.

At HQS, there is a row of three trees beside the front entrance. Each is dedicated to a different Soviet asset, still unnamed, who shared that kind of relationship with the operative who handled them. Each played their unsung role in preventing nuclear war. Without them, none of us might be here at all. Their courage is the reason the training is so hard. If we screw up, they pay the price, and with every passing day, I see more classmates learn the cost of one of their mistakes. A bullet in their asset's head as he sits at a red light. A photo of their child bound and killed. All fake, of course, in this world of training pretend, but real enough to lodge deep in my amygdala, real enough to replace roadblocks and prison and torture to become the greatest fear of all.

Students who lose an asset also lose their place at the Farm. For the rest of us, the recruitment cycle continues. Next comes running—the long sweeping arc of a source's working relationship with the Agency. For years, sometimes even decades, an asset is run in place—asked to remain in their current job or even progress to a level of greater access, where they can answer the questions our analysts send and warn us of impending attacks. Those questions, known as "requirements," arrive to us field officers via long cables, jampacked with clinical-sounding terms and potentially offensive assumptions. It's our job to pick and choose the most important, massage them into palatable queries, and raise them during our next car meeting or hotel debrief with the source. All our meetings at this post-recruitment stage are clandestine. Arranged via predetermined signals, which are themselves documented for HQS, to ensure that a new field officer could take over an asset in case we disappear, or worse.

We learn these signaling and meeting

techniques as we go, with new ones added during each exercise. There are the traditional chalk marks and lowered window blinds, shifts in the physical world made by one of us in a place the other can see during their daily commute. Then there are the newer, more creative ideas. One instructor prefers using Starbucks gift cards. They have a balance he can check by typing the card number into the Starbucks website. He gives one to each of his assets and tells them, "If you need to see me, buy a coffee." Then he checks the card numbers on a cybercafé computer each day, and if the balance on one is depleted, he knows he's got a meeting. Saves him having to drive past a whole slew of different physical signal sites each day. And the card numbers aren't tied to identities, so the whole thing is pretty secure. I like it. But some of the older instructors don't. We learn quickly which Cold War veterans demand chalk marks from their students and which modern warriors prefer silicon and Wi-Fi.

When an asset signals for a meeting, we head to a predetermined spot—an operational site we've cased and scouted, checking to be sure it fulfills the slew of attributes our instructors have drilled into us with endless lists of acronyms. Something as simple as a car pickup site—the spot where an asset knows to stand so we can swoop in and scoop them up—must be shielded from passersby, have a separate entrance and exit, be free of cameras and security personnel, sit sufficiently far from hot spots like police stations or schools, remain accessible twenty-four hours a day, and offer some plausible explanation for why somebody of the asset's position or stature would be hanging around alone, often in the wee hours of morning.

Given all the care that's gone into selecting the pickup spot, it wouldn't do to take a tail to the meeting, so we can't drive straight there. Instead, we embark on long, circuitous surveillance detection routes, known as SDRs. The aim is to identify cars or people who keep popping up over time and distance. If we see the same granny with a yoga mat twice on the same street, she could just be walking in the same direction we are. But see her twice on two different streets, miles and hours apart, and we might have just nailed our surveillant. To spice things up, surveillants work in teams of seven or eight, switching off with one another each time we turn left or right, so that no single surveillant is exposed more than a handful of times over the entire route. It's a cat-and-mouse labyrinth chase through city streets, and the only way to win is to design a route with enough changes of direction to force surveillance to stick close. Better yet, add in a few stops at a shopping mall or subway station with multiple entrances and exits, to be sure they have to follow us inside on foot. All the while, we have to look nonalerting—just out for a boring old afternoon of errands. Which means designing routes where every change of direction is anchored by some plausible visit to a store or a gym or a mechanic. And ideally those cover stops have to make sense both day and night, because there's no way in advance to know when an asset will signal for a meeting.

All that need for pickup spots and surveillance detection routes means that our every unoccupied minute of time at the Farm is spent casing the surrounding area for operational sites.

"When I retire," Dave jokes, "I'm coming back down here to open a restaurant that just happens to have perfect cover and flow. Guaranteed business from every class of students."

When a source loses their access or just gets to a point where they prefer to call it a day, the recruitment cycle reaches its last stop: terminate. This isn't the termination you hear about in the movies—the kind with quotation marks around it and blood splatter on the walls. These are dignified, intensely emotional conversations about the end of an era, about gratitude and honor and legacy. Sometimes the source knows they're finished even when the case officer wishes they'd continue. Sometimes it's the other way around. But more often than not, it's a decision they make together, two long-bound dogs of war who know when the battle is through. There's no way to fully prepare for these terminations when they happen in the field after decades of shared risk and reward. But even in the abbreviated timeline of our year at the Farm, the terminations are the hardest—good-byes to the few people who know and share our truth.

After each exercise at every step of the cycle, we retreat to our SCIF and write a fake cable to HQS describing the interaction. This is the part of the training—the part of the job—that doesn't make the spy novels. The paperwork kingdom. Cables describing a person of interest, applications for clearance to pursue, requests for traces, descriptions of each subsequent contact, coordination of the approach to recruit, validation that the target doesn't work for an adversary, permissions from liaison governments. And then, once the target's been recruited, the constant exchange of requirements written by analysts or policy makers back home.

We type them up on secure computers. At the top we add the distro—a list of stations in relevant cities that have a stake in the asset or the topic at hand. We add slugs, code words that identify the cable's subject matter and allow those with access to find it in the Agency's classified search. And we slap on the classification itself, a single judgment call that for all time determines who will be able to read our words and when.

In real life, the cables are submitted via secure Internet, if written in a station, or via covert communications devices, if written by a NOC in the field. But here at the Farm, we print them out on good old-fashioned printer paper and hand-deliver them to our instructors' mailboxes in the central lecture hall.

With ever more exercises underway, the hour when we finish our daily cables grows later and later. There's a peace to the Farm at night, when the day's humidity has settled and the hum of distant traffic gives way to insect song. There are bikes parked at each building, to be picked up and dropped off at random. They give the place a nostalgic feel, sending me back to the time Christian and I cut up cereal boxes and wedged the cardboard in our spokes to sound like motors. Each night, I print out the last of my cables and saddle up whichever bike looks least likely to lose its chain. I push off under the streetlight, its form oddly Dickensian, like Tumnus's lamp in Narnia. Alternately pedaling and coasting, I listen to my breath merge with the wind, and surrender to the vastness of the woods and the mission and the sky. This is the only moment of the day when I am alone. The air is alive, and I am proud and tired and free. Then before I've even properly started, I am there, outside the lecture hall, pressing my day's work into a pigeonhole and winding my way toward sleep.

The pace of our training ramps up exponentially as the weeks pass. One exercise each Monday in January becomes four or five a day by June. We add land navigation, trekking for days across woods and cliffs to meet our assets, armed with nothing more than a map in a ziplock bag, a compass, and a rainproof notebook. We learn defensive driving, our instructors teaching us to flip cars by tapping a spot above their rear wheel with our own front grill and how to respond in seconds when swarmed by armed militia fighters or trapped at an ambush. They leave fake roadside bombs around campus for us to identify; we indicate that we've found one by pulling over and popping our trunk. Fail to do so and they assume we would have been toast, which means that as far as the Farm is concerned, we are.

Toward the end of the course, we begin to mix in weapons qualifications. Glock and M4. Training in urban-combat scenarios, the faux city blocks stocked with dummies—some legitimate targets, most dressed as local men, women, or children. Hit a civilian and we're out. Even the actual targets have to be given first aid as soon as we complete our objective or the compound is secured. It's not clear if the point of that policy is compassion or to keep the adversary alive for interrogation, but there's something confusingly tender about it, the nursing of wounds we ourselves have just inflicted. We learn to use tourniquets to stem the bleeding and to cover sucking chest wounds with supermarket bags, duct-taped to a patient's skin as their pierced lung heaves beneath.

"Excellent work," an instructor tells me at the end of an exercise in responding to a checkpoint ambush. I look down at my target dummy. His tunic is soaked with blood and ripped open from throat to navel. Across his chest is a plastic bag, with "Wal-Mart" taped over his heart.

11

At the end of our stay at the Farm, on a day we don't know is coming, a siren blares across the base. It means the simulation is over. The explosions stop. The interrogations shut down. The instructors playing terrorists and cabinet members get up mid-meeting and walk away.

We just stand there for a minute, in the deadened aftermath of the fake town square, like survivors of an apocalyptic event, unsure what to do now that our world has evaporated. And then a two-day period of limbo kicks in. It's been weeks since we've had time to ourselves. But we don't fall into one another the way we normally do. We split off, alone. Uncertain whether we've made the cut, uncertain whether it was all for nothing. And if we did make it, even then, what was it for? To leave one simulation and go play in another?

It's unnerving, how suddenly the game of pretend can end. So all-encompassing one day, with flash-bangs and police checkpoints and survival on the line, then suddenly over the next, with nothing but the peaceful breeze on the water remaining—the bare, wooden stage that outlasts the play. I ask myself, sitting by the lake, how we could sound a siren to end the real war game the way this morning's blast ended our training one.

At the end of that strange, solitary two days, I wander into the town square and find a man I've never met sitting in the gazebo. "You're in my spot," I tell him. He just smiles and says, "Dean Fox." I stare at him for a minute and say, "I was gonna hit up the beer machine. You want one?"

Two hours later, we get called in to hear our respective fates. We both make it. His envelope says, "Afghanistan." Mine says, "See Dan." I show Dean. "Never heard of that country," I say. He smiles. "It's next to Chad," he says. Africa nerd humor. Be still my beating heart.

I go to see Dan, my training branch chief. He tells me I've been pulled out to be under nonofficial cover—one of the hardest and most coveted assignments in the class. Most

CIA operatives deploy under diplomatic cover, pretending to be a low-level secretary at the U.S. embassy by day and working their espionage targets at night. That's fine for Cold War–style spycraft, recruiting members of foreign governments, but terror cells don't much care whether someone is a U.S. diplomat or a U.S. spy—if they work for the U.S. government, they're a target. To infiltrate terror networks, you need a different kind of cover altogether. Businesswoman, artist, or aid worker, I'll need to work out the details of a cover that fits my profile and my mission once I report back to HQS following training. For now, I try to let the significance of the designation sink in.

Dan pours me a drink. Nonofficial cover is an honor, he tells me, but it's no picnic. It means I won't have diplomatic immunity. No all-important official passport to bail me out of trouble like a golden "Get Out of Jail Free" card tucked safely in my pocket. No comfort of working in an embassy every day, surrounded by people who share my truth. I'll be alone, without a safety net, in the most dangerous places the planet has to offer. But I'll have the best shot at doing what I signed up to do: preventing the most catastrophic attacks.

Dan sends me outside to pack into the van

with the others who made the cut and I'm flying, not sure where I end and they begin. We're on our way across the vast wilderness of the base to a lone covert airstrip, where we'll become the newest graduates of the most challenging operational training on earth. Someone blares "The Final Countdown" on the stereo. Everyone is singing. I slide the window open and the air is hot and fast and my heart is outside of me. Then we arrive at an airplane hangar full of chairs, with an American flag hung over the stage. The director arrives by helicopter, and one by one, we cross the stage, shake his hand, and lay fleeting eyes on the diplomas we're not allowed to take home.

A sunset, a sunrise, and a lot of alcohol later, we pack up our fictional lives and head back to D.C., dozing in happy exhaustion in the darkened warmth of the blacked-out bus.

Amid the cookie-cutter condos of Arlington I brace myself to face reality in the form of Anthony. But I find our apartment empty, a few remaining things in boxes, and a note that says our cat is at the local humane society.

Anthony is gone. And in the stillness, I'm flooded with relief.

—

I'm assigned back to CTC/WMD, charged once again with keeping nuclear, biological, and chemical agents out of the hands of global terror groups. I'm working operations around the world and returning only to switch out bags, pick up new alias docs, and get a fitful night's sleep between briefings.

After a few months, my boss calls me into his office and says it's time to pick a more permanent cover. The Beltway consultancy gig is fine for friends and family—even for customs and passport officials in the countries I'm visiting—but it carries too much D.C. stigma to allow me to get close to the top targets we're pursuing. Up until now, I've been debriefing detainees or working with our counterparts in allied governments to plan or monitor operations. But if I want to be recruiting and running terrorist assets myself, I need a cover story that doesn't reek of Washington.

"You're a twenty-five-year-old white girl," he says. "Don't hide from that. Lean into it. What reason could you possibly have for being in Yemen or Libya or the North-West Frontier Province of Pakistan?"

There's aid work, but that cover has been used a thousand times before. And each time it is, it erodes the ability of real aid workers to do their job without falling under local suspicion. There's journalism and documentary filmmaking, a nod to my history freelancing in Thailand and Burma. But that cover holds for only so long, until it becomes obvious that your work isn't showing up on the wires.

"What about art?" I ask.

"Go on."

My parents collect it, I explain. My sister is studying it. Anyone would believe I'd be drawn into that world, too. With artists from emerging scenes like China and India making record sales at Sotheby's and Christie's, it would make total sense for a young entrepreneur to be out scouting new markets in the Middle East, Asia, and Africa. If China's anything to go by, I say, governments and criminals alike love using the art scene to launder money, so there's real access there. It might even allow me to brush up against some antiquities dealers hawking war trophies. Most of all, it would give me a reason to run around the boonies with sealed boxes and bags.

He mulls this over for a minute, then nods.

"Sold. Family history makes it believable. And the art market's just dirty enough to give you entrée to the netherworld when you need it. Get it set up."

It turns out that "getting it set up" involves hundreds of hours of work. There's the preparation of fake business plans and financials to ensure that I can talk mechanics if anyone should ask. There's designing the website and creating the digital litter—search results that reinforce the company's legitimacy. There's the printing of business cards—my own and those of colleagues I would have met were this my real job. There's the forging of expired conference passes to scatter in my backpack and the generation of a year's past e-mail traffic with nonexistent correspondents, in case anyone should check my phone or hack my digital accounts. It's the birthing of an entire identity, all to backstop one simple line: "I deal in indigenous art."

Alongside the creation of my cover, I have a few other post-Farm errands to run. I stop by the Directorate of Science and Technology, known as the DS&T, to design my covcom—the covert communications system I'll use to communicate with HQS from the field. Most operatives rely on secure computers in the embassy's station to send their cables, but as a NOC, I won't step foot in the embassy door. For us nonofficial types, the DS&T teams design systems that can travel with us, embedded in our computers and accessed through labyrinthine combinations of physical trapdoors and online keystrokes to be sure no inspecting customs officer can find them. Each is created from scratch with a given NOC's cover in mind, and now that I have the art business underway, it's time to get my covcom fired up to match.

I sit with the engineers in their warehouse of technical delights and brief them on the finer points of my new business. They scribble notes with a pencil—the only low-tech item in the room—and, a few weeks later, present me with a phone and a long list of instructions, to be carried out in the correct order to unlock the covcom hidden inside. There are buttons and switches interspersed with keystrokes and visits to art-related web-sites and edits to pictures of the Louvre. It's a spy-tech Konami code, like the combinations of commands that unlocked secret power-ups in the Nintendo games we played when we were kids. There's a cheekiness to it, hiding a portal to the heart of the government's secrets right there in plain sight of every adversary I'll meet. I tuck it away like a Batphone, my secret connection to the cavalry back home. It is my talisman. It makes me feel less alone.

Down the hall in the DS&T is an alto-gether different room, hung with fabrics and leathers and lace. It is the CD shop, where tailoring wizards add concealment devices to briefcases and dresses and coats. They've pulled a Tumi bag in preparation for our meeting. "These are my favorites," the woman tells me. "Professional, anonymous, well-heeled but not luxurious." I grimace at its plush smugness.

"Do you have anything a bit more hippie-backpacker save-the-world art lover?" I ask.

The woman smiles. "Stand by," she says and disappears into the fabrics. When she reemerges she's holding a woven cloth hobo bag, straight out of a Thai night market.

"Bingo," I say, and she winks.

When I return to pick it up, she walks me through the three compartments she's added, each of a different size, and accessed through its own particular combination of thread tugs and flap pulls.

"Magic," I say.

"Just a regular old Muggle," she says. "Doing my best."

The last tech stop is a few floors up, in a mirrored makeup studio hung with latex noses and glasses and wigs. I'm there to be fitted for light disguise—a ridiculous getup, not much better than a drugstore Halloween costume, intended to throw surveillance off the trail during a testing SDR.

"I'm not sure anyone's gonna buy this," I say to the man as he stuffs the last of my hair under a '60s bob.

"It's for from far away," he says in a French accent. "Try these." He adds a pair of spectacles. They are more preposterous than the wig, but somehow the combined effect cancels out to an awkward but nonalerting librarian.

"Fine," I say. "Can't imagine using these, to be honest, but seems as good a getup as any if I have to."

The man looks miffed but tags them with my Agency ID number and pads off to find some clay to make a mold of my face. I'm pretty sure he leaves me caked in the stuff a beat longer than he has to, lying on my back and breathing through a straw. "Don't piss off Guillaume," I remember my boss telling me when I spotted a crooked latex nose hanging from his cabinet. Now I understand what he meant.

Reality gets more and more distant, obscured by the ever-thicker veil of my new cover. I take my first trip under its protection and then my second. At the beginning, I run through the details obsessively during each flight, preparing for possible grilling at customs when I land. But soon I come to slip in and out of it more easily, like a softening pair of shoes.

The real world feels farther and farther away. My annulment with Anthony is finalized, and the papers sit in an unopened envelope on my kitchen table.

I go to brunch with my family at a café on the Potomac River and tell them I'm going to try my hand at dealing in indigenous art. They don't take much convincing. They'd never understood why I'd wanted to work for a multinational anyway. Seeking out cultural expression in far-off lands is a much better match with their expectations of me.

"Now, that's the Burma rebel I know and love," my sister chimes in. I'm relieved when they buy it. If they do, maybe al Qa'ida will, too.

"Just don't get thrown in prison," my mother jokes.

"Not much chance of that," I laugh. Of all the lies I tell them, that one is the biggest.

I see Dean on the rare occasions when we're both home. He's finishing up some paramilitary courses, getting ready to pack out to Afghanistan. I'm mostly at airports between this identity and that one. He doesn't know much about my work, and I don't know much about his. There is a closeness in the way we both accept our distance. He seems to understand where he fits in the multilevel game of pretend. Somewhere closer to the truth than my family, who thinks I'm out collecting tribal art, and further away than my boss in the safe house, who hands me sealed envelopes I have to sign before I can read what's inside them.

Dean's growing a beard to prepare for deployment to the Pak-Afghan border. It will be his only armor out there, and I can already feel it at work here at home, protecting him from getting too attached to me. Still, we laugh and drink and walk Kipling, my giant White Fang of a dog, along the Georgetown canals. Before he leaves, I give him a box of little envelopes, each with a different date on the front, one a week for six months. Inside each one is some silly drawing or joke. Then I drive him to the private air terminal at Dulles and watch him climb onto a blacked-out chartered jet to the mountains of Afghanistan.

It helps, having him gone. My ops are ramping up, and I need to focus. Most of my classmates are deploying under diplomatic cover, posing as State Department staffers behind the impermeable walls and guard posts of embassies and military outposts. I'm working without immunity and without the comfort or guidance of colleagues around me. Just me and my covcom, through which I receive bare-bones instructions from desk people at HQS, most of whom I've never met. And while I'm growing accustomed to that isolation, Dean is getting used to his Afghan forward operating base (FOB), where things couldn't be more different. Instead of learning how to blend deeper into his cover, he's learning to clear compounds (euphemism for "kill the men inside"), wearing night-vision goggles and extra rounds for his M4. Once a **National Geographic** photographer, he's now sizing things up through a different kind of lens.

We write each other letters about small things. The trick he's taught a dog to do in the green zone. The flowers that are taking hold in my yard. There's something old-fashioned about it. A World War II kind of a romance, contained in words on a page—words that are about nothing, and somehow also about everything.

Every so often, during those two years of constant operations, he gets a chunk of R&R leave and I schedule a gap between missions and we meet somewhere, in Honduras or the Bahamas, and greedily inhale each other for days of blind release. Then he gets back on a chartered flight to the badlands and I take off for a meeting in some foreign café, and we both look away from the feeling that we don't know each other much better than we did that first day in the gazebo. Increasingly often every time he returns, he grapples with me violently in his sleep. But his kiss in the morning is kind, and we let each other battle our respective demons in peace.

12

Dean is away for three months at a time, calling me at weird sunrise hours, full of stories about the monkeys they've adopted on the base or the pranks they've pulled while out on patrol. He never mentions the fighting. Never lets slip any suggestion that his life is in danger, out beyond the blast walls that protect his bed from bombs. Once a week or so, the phone line goes dead as we're talking and my bedroom is plunged back into quiet. Every time, I know it's probably the satellite. Every time, I wonder if it's incoming fire.

He sends photographs by e-mail. An old man asleep beside his market stall, piled with laundry detergent and rifles. A gaggle of boys passing a clay pipe, one inhaling as another doubles over to cough. A secret girls' school, its rows of hijabed heads bent over their math problems. These are glimpses of life under the Taliban. And glimpses of Dean's true self, filled with a tenderness he cannot or will not express in words. I love him for seeing these strangers so clearly, even as he fights for survival in their midst.

Far less often, he sends pictures of his own reflection. The first is in a suction-cup mirror, stuck to the wall of the shipping container he's assigned to sleep in when he initially arrives on base. He's tall and rangy, with tousled hair and boyish softness around his eyes. His skin is smooth and clean, his eyes bright, mischievous. He doesn't send another for nine weeks. Then, suddenly, there he is again, bearded and hunched, Ray-Bans over his eyes and an M4 slung across his chest. He's standing in a row of other men, each similarly dressed and armed. The boy in him is gone.

I stare at their masked eyes. They are Dean's family now. Together, they do their CrossFit. Together, they clock their kills. It's hard to tell them apart.

One of the men I know from the Farm. His name is Matt. His girlfriend is a friend of mine. He's still married to someone else, as it turns out. He says it's only paperwork. He'll sort it all out when he gets home from war. Then he sends me a picture of his penis. And before I can decide what to do with my outrage, he gets shot on an evening patrol.

I'm not prepared for it, not ready for a classmate of mine—even a slimy one—to be gunned down in combat. It's not the CIA's job to play special forces, to get into firefights on the soil of foreign wars. CIA operatives aren't optimized for combat. We have the military for that. Billions of dollars and more than a million men and women, deployed for that very purpose. At their best, Agency officers are charged with a different kind of defense: the act of listening, learning, building relationships, cultivating trust. It's soulful work, investing in a relationship with the adversary. Only in times of great military strain do graduates of the Farm get asked to forgo that work in favor of the trenches. "The surge," as this period is now known, is one of those times.

It's a punch in the gut for a Farm graduate to get surged to a war zone. Too many months clearing compounds in Humvees with air support and night vision begins to erode the subtle training that enables operatives to move from cocktail party to terror-cell safe house without a trace. More than a year or two in combat, and they might as well not have been through the Farm at all. I hate that Dean got chosen. I can see why: his agility and temperament and skill. But it isn't what he signed up for, these midnight raids and his trigger finger throbbing with kill or be killed.

CIA operatives lose their lives, too, of course—the stars on the wall are reminder enough of that—but the danger we face is different. It's our cover and not our weapon that keeps us from being killed. It's our adversary's trust and not his scalp we seek. Soldiers see a problem and try to destroy it. Intelligence officers see a problem and try to befriend it. That is, until they get surged to Afghanistan and shot on an evening patrol.

Matt lives, but it's a reminder of the incoming fire Dean faces, the danger he tries to mask each time we talk. It's wearing to care about someone who gets shot at every day. And the only way I know how to cope is by diving headlong into work.

The focus isn't hard to muster, given the weekly drumbeat of intelligence suggesting that the threat of a nuclear attack is inevitable, even imminent. For decades, brokers around the world have traded WMD precursors and components, some fueled by a Machiavellian focus on power and money, others driven by the belief that every country should have the same right to a national defense. Nuclear weapons, their argument goes, should be either permitted or banned, with all nation-states abiding by the same rule. It's a compelling piece of logic, except that leaders who already have the bomb show no sign of disarming, and a world where every country has a nuclear arsenal doesn't feel terribly secure. Still, many object to the Western world's "bomb for the rich, no bomb for the poor" approach and, whether in pursuit of equanimity or a comfortable retirement, several have made a healthy business out of hawking black-market and dual-use components to governments seeking a nuclear arsenal of their own.

As I get settled at the safe house again, the most famous of these networks, led by a Pakistani metallurgist named Abdul Qadeer Khan, is in the process of being dismantled. The reports we're getting from the resulting debriefings suggest that it isn't just nation-states his people have been supplying. The Khan network has operated with something close to impunity for over twenty years, masterminding the Pakistani nuclear program before going increasingly rogue to supply Libya, Iran, and North Korea with centrifuge designs and components in exchange for the cash and uranium required to make the Pakistani system tick. Then along came the interception of a ship carrying Khan-supplied technology to Libya, followed by Colonel Muammar Qaddafi's offer to unilaterally dismantle his nuclear program to avoid military fallout. All of a sudden, A. Q. Khan is on the defensive and the brokers who've been dealing on his behalf are beginning to talk.

We receive a quickening influx of cables suggesting that Pakistan's pursuit of the "Islamic bomb" didn't stop at trade with rogue governments. In enough cases to be worrying, brokers report being approached by al Qa'ida itself.

With the ramp-up in threat reporting, we get a firehose of funding and personnel. Our CTC/WMD safe house expands to occupy a second floor of the nondescript office building that provides its cover. Like the floor below, this one has a normal glass-fronted reception area, where visitors are screened for clearance, then sent back down a hallway to drop off phones and other transmitting devices before passing through two SCIF doors and into a floor-sized safe. I move upstairs to focus on the brokers who survived the Khan roundup only to form a spin-off network selling to terror groups instead. We coordinate with the teams dismantling supply to the state programs, but our responsibility is strictly nonstate actors, from al Qa'ida to the apocalyptic end-of-days cults that pop up periodically in a horrific spasm of violence, like the Jonestown massacre or the Aum Shinrikyo sarin attack on the Tokyo subway system in 1995.

I get up to speed on what we know by visiting detainees in Europe and Asia who are awaiting trial for their role in Khan's reign of global proliferation. I ask them about sales to terror groups. Most avoid the question, but one—a Swede—makes no apologies.

"Dr. Khan committed his life to leveling the playing field," he says in precise English. "He saw his country humiliated by India on the battlefield. Then he himself was humiliated by an Indian soldier on a train crossing the Pakistani border. The soldier took his favorite pen. It wasn't a big thing. But he did it because he could get away with it."

"So because someone took his favorite pen, he decided to help terrorists build a nuclear bomb," I say. It sounds snarky, even to me.

He cocks his head slightly, as if assessing me. Then he shrugs. "Humiliation is a powerful thing," he says, without judgment. "Nuclear weapons are just a stand-in for respect. Everyone wants respect, wouldn't you say? Even the people you call terrorists."

We let the silence sit for a minute. He's not wrong. But the truth doesn't absolve the crime.

"They call you terrorists, by the way," he adds as an afterthought.

On the way home, at Frankfurt Airport, I watch a boy watch security officers search his mother's hijab. I think of the time I saw a banker repossessing a home drop a woman's house keys into the garbage. Her kid had made the key ring. It clanged when it hit the metal base. A few months later, I read a newspaper article about a banker's murder, and part of me understood. Ants flee the stomping boot of power. Until, one day, they don't. The Swede leaves me unsettled. Loose nukes combined with humiliated humans doesn't end well for anyone.

I get back to the safe house and start mapping the brokers on a conference room wall. The more I flesh out each node, the more I realize that the fall of Khan's network isn't diminishing the potential for nuclear terrorism. If anything, it's intensifying it. Dealers who once sold their wares to Qaddafi and Kim now have space on their dance cards for al-Zawahiri and bin Laden. I present these findings to my boss, and he drops a box of files on the conference room table.

"No shit," he says.

Inside are folders—dozens of credible nuclear threats since 2001. I'd known about the Dragonfire incident—an intelligence report the month after 9/11 suggesting that al Qa'ida had a ten-kiloton nuclear weapon stashed somewhere in New York City. The source, an Agency asset encrypted as Dragonfire, was deemed credible enough that the vice president and an entire shadow government were moved to an undisclosed location for more than a month in case D.C. got vaporized. So far, that hasn't happened, but given the other folders in this box, it seems it's not for lack of trying. Report after report refers to "a nuclear reckoning" or an "American Hiroshima." Al Qa'ida clerics call for the death of four million Americans to pay for the Muslim civilians they claim U.S. policies have killed. Humans have only one technology capable of achieving those numbers, and it's shaped like a mushroom cloud.

My boss watches me as I read.

"Hard to unsee, huh?" he asks. I nod. "We've been in triage mode. Focused on preventing attacks once they're already planned. But we should be playing the long game, too. I just got a couple of newbies from the latest crop at the Farm. Take them, if you want. See if you can't cut some of this off at the point of supply."

At twenty-six, I'm suddenly managing two new operatives and an administrative desk officer, along with a slew of support staff. We're impossibly young to have the fate of the world in our hands. But such is the way of the Agency. By thirty-five, any operative worth their salt has gone hard enough at their job to erode their cover. My chief explained it to me once in training: "You could sit in a closet for twenty years and your cover would remain pristine, but you wouldn't have saved a single life. Get out there. Recruit assets. Stop attacks. After a while, someone's gonna call you out. But that's better than never doing anything at all." He raised his coffee like a cocktail. "Remember, kid, if you're gonna fall, fall forward."

Once an operative's cover is eroded, they can still work. They run our bases and stations around the world or come back to manage branches at home. But the undercover, tip-of-the-spear, real-deal case officers are the youngest of the bunch. That's us. With our pristine cover, a whole lot of swagger, and zero real-world experience between us.

We're tasked with mapping the tentacles of the network and preventing nuclear precursors from actually changing hands. At first, we tackle this by posing as buyers. I ask one of my new guys, Neil, to comb through the message intercepts, ranking each seller's responsiveness to new customers. Neil's an MIT PhD—the type of charming genius who would have been equally at home banging out code for the NSA as he is working diplomatic cocktail parties for us. He takes over my upper-floor conference room map, circling known sellers of nuclear precursors in red and ranking buyers by the depth and credibility of their follow-on connections.

The more qualified buyers a seller has, the better his access to terror groups of interest, but the less he needs new customers and the lower the likelihood that our approach would make it to a meeting. The ideal target is a seller with links to more established brokers but too few buyers of his own. Find a guy like that and we have a shot at setting up a meeting, only to daisy-chain the low-level dealer into contact with a higher-level guy once we get our foot in the door. One seller in particular, a Hungarian named Jakab, has links to the best brokers in the business but still responds to almost every inquiry he receives.

"Hustlers gonna hustle," Neil says. "Looks

like maybe he's an apprentice to the big guys trying to go out on his own."

We strategize about how best to approach him, taking breaks to hit up Chipotle and Panda Express, down beneath our tower of safety, surrounded by lunch-break shoppers in skirt suits and sneakers.

"Lucy Stanton?" a rosacea-cheeked woman approaches the mother sitting next to us in the outdoor food court one day. The mom looks uninterested. "I'm a friend of Jen's," the ruddy-faced woman persists. "She suggested I talk to you about playgroup." Suddenly the mom's face brightens. She picks up her youngest to make room for the rosy-cheeked stranger to sit down. Neil turns to me.

"That's it. We need someone to refer us," he says. "We need a Jen."

I nod into my iced tea. Nobody likes a stranger.

"Do we have any friends who might oblige?" I ask.

"Maybe Kite Wing." It's a risky business, mentioning crypts out here in the open. On the off chance that our safe house cover has been blown, there could be foreign government surveillants around us. Sniffing out CIA operatives is a favorite pastime of our young, hungry counterparts, posted to the Russian embassy across the Potomac in D.C. Even our own security officers have been known to check up on fellow operatives, ensuring that classified information remains in the four walls of a SCIF.

I give Neil a scowl. But he's not wrong. Kite Wing is the cryptonym for a longtime asset in the upper echelons of Hizb'allah, the Shi'ite terror group funded by Iran that passes itself off as a community organization in Lebanon and beyond. It's a shrewd suggestion. Hizb'allah has limited contact with the Sunni groups we're after, the al Qa'idas and Jemaah Islamiyahs of the world. That means little risk that he'd want to blow our cover. If anything, he'd like to see the Sunni groups wiped from the proverbial map. Our objectives are pretty well aligned. And a referral from one of Hizb'allah's top lieutenants should all but guarantee that Jakab takes us seriously.

Still, Neil shouldn't be using crypts in public.

He smiles back at me, a "Yeah, but am I right" smile that I can't help but return. It's a good feeling to have cracked this thing, here at a plastic-coated picnic table between the food stalls and Ross Dress for Less.

"Okay, okay. Let's just take it upstairs," I say.

"That's what she said," he quips back, in

case I'd forgotten that we're only playacting at adulthood.

"Keep it classy, Neil."

He crumples his burrito wrapper and shoots for the garbage bin—slam dunk—then tips an imaginary hat in my direction.

"Yes, ma'am. Right after I get done saving the world."

13

Neil's plan works. Kite Wing introduces me as a broker for the "Southeast Asian brothers," a characterization sufficiently vague to confer credibility while still leaving me enough flexibility to craft the details myself. Like so many of his more connected colleagues, Jakab communicates mostly by using the Drafts folder of an e-mail account. Write a message, save it to Drafts, ensure that your recipient has the account's e-mail address and password, and wait for him or her to log in and read it. The recipient then leaves their reply in the same folder, all without ever having to actually send a message—a crude but successful attempt to get around the e-mail intercepts dealers fear most.

On Kite Wing's vouching, Jakab sets up an e-mail address to contact me for a meeting.

When I get the details, I can't help shaking my head. GeneralRipperB52@hotmail.com. General Jack Ripper. The crazed U.S. Air Force officer who initiates a first nuclear strike in the movie **Dr. Strangelove.** Evidently, we have a film buff on our hands.

Jakab and I dance around each other in the Drafts folder for almost a month; I inquire about tools of elevated efficacy and use a host of other known euphemisms for nuclear and biological weapons. Several times, he demurs.

"Our mutual friend mentioned you might be able to provide my buyers with such technology," I press.

"Would appreciate if you could clarify in person," he replies.

I arrange to meet him a few weeks later in Lyon, a bacchanalian French city with a penchant for all things joie de vivre. It's a strange place to find a man who aspires to deal in death, what with the music drifting from the park as the day goes to gloaming and the laughter issuing from pretty, wine-stained mouths along the riverbank. But it was his suggestion, and I have no reason to object. Might as well let him think he's on home turf.

I can see him, a few dozen yards ahead of

me, on his way to our meeting. He's wearing a canvas barn coat and leather boots that rise to midcalf. From behind, he has the gait of a western farmhand. I can't tell, until he turns onto a side street, that he is singing. But as soon as the sound hits me, I soften. The tune is an old folk song, the kind that makes people feel nostalgic, even if they've never heard it before. His voice is grandfatherly and sorrowful, older than I expected, wiser than his e-mail posturing let on.

I get ready to bump him. It's a security measure, finding a way to stage a brief encounter with a new target before he knows it's me he's talking to. As far as Jakab's concerned, I'm waiting for him at a café a few streets over. Safer to approach him here, though, when he's not expecting it. Targets tend to choose familiar locations for initial meetings—places where people know them. Intercepting him at a point of my choosing allows me to control the environment and get both his hands where I can see them before he knows our meeting's even started.

"Excusez-moi," I say as I touch his elbow. "Tu as du feu?" I hold out an unlit cigarette. He turns and nods gruffly. I'm startled at how little his face resembles his voice. Gone is the paternal image in my mind's eye, replaced with a brutish rectangle of a man, young and thick, all angular sinew like a Stalinist statue with prison tattoos. He retrieves a dented metal lighter from his breast pocket and flicks it a few times before it takes. The air between us smells of petrol. I dip the end of my cigarette into the flame and look up at his face.

"Jakab, yes?" I say.

His hands are still in midair. He looks startled.

"I recognized you from our mutual friend's description," I continue. "Pleasure to meet you." I'm pumping his hand up and down before he's fully registered what I'm saying. "I have a car just here. Shall we get out of the cold?"

I walk toward a rented VW I've parked across the street and don't turn around, just get in and shut the driver's door. It's ballsy, considering the amount of work that's gone into getting him here and the possibility of scaring him off, but there's no point in giving him the chance to argue. Better to wait for him in the car. This way he only has two choices—accept the change of plans or risk losing a sale—and neither option involves a public conversation, which will be critical if I want to recruit him down the road.

When I finally look back, he's still standing there, watching me from the far side of the cobblestones. He looks curious, even bemused. Twenty-six-year-old girls don't often play in the arms dealing game. He lights a cigarette of his own, then walks across the street. When the passenger door is closed behind him, I turn on the engine to crack the windows. Charlie Parker is playing his saxophone on the radio.

"Mind if we drive?" I ask.

"You don't look like a sand nigger," he says.

"I work with a lot of folks," I answer, hiding my disgust at his language.

"Why?" he asks. He still hasn't answered my original question, so I pull out of the parking spot and begin driving down the street. I'm pushing the limits of his comfort zone; I can feel it. But I want to get us off the X—move us away from the danger zone. It's never a good idea to stay in a meeting spot too long. A few turns and we'll be clear of anyone he might have made arrangements with to cover his back.

"Because I'm a businesswoman," I say, "and businesspeople don't see black or white."

He looks at me, then out the rear window, then back at me.

"Only green," he says.

"I prefer to think of it as only opportunity." I turn onto the main boulevard, then dogleg onto another side street. "And right now, I have an opportunity that stands to make both of us some money. Depending on what you have available."

It's clumsy. I should have waited—let him be the one to turn the talk to trade. Advantage always belongs to the respondent.

"Pistols, assault weapons, all manner of military surplus," he says and taps his ashes through the cracked window. He's giving me his cover story. Nothing even remotely approaching the world of WMD precursors on that list. I kick myself for charging too hard. But there's no backing off now.

"My buyers are looking for something more efficient," I say. "They can pay."

"I don't think I know what you mean," he says and flicks his cigarette out the window. "You can drop me here."

I steady myself against the temptation to backtrack. I think about the months that have gone into this operation, the other assets we've involved, all to get to this moment. I think about telling my boss I blew it. I think about turning on the news to hear that there's been an attack. I think about failing. And I want to beg him not to get out of the car. But

I'm locked on course now. The only way out is through.

"Sorry to hear that," I say and pull over. "Our mutual friend misunderstood your access."

He stares at me for a long moment. Then he gets out of the car, and I drive away.

So much for the Farm. So much for training. So much for the best and the brightest. I'm an idiot. I got cocky, and it might cost more than I can bear. I park in the public transit lot and do a surveillance detection route back to my hotel. Then I order a whiskey.

—

When I get back to D.C., my boss lets me brief him on the whole sorry story before he tells me that Jakab left a message in the Drafts folder that morning. "Says he has something that might fit the bill," he notes. I feel the grin wash over me. "But you're still an idiot," he adds.

Thank God today Jakab happens to be a bigger one.

I send the reply to my boss for approval before I save it to Jakab's Drafts. It's polite but curt: "Have found a different supplier for this order. Will circle back the next time I have a need." Then I go silent. He reaches out a few weeks later. And again after a month.

"Sounds like he's in need of some scratch," Neil says.

"Guess the question is, What do we do with him?" I say. "We could just start buying everything he has to sell. Keep it off the market. But eventually he's going to get wise to the fact that we're not selling it on. Buyers talk."

"Worth it in the meantime?" Neil asks. "If he's got access to former Soviet research facilities—and from the intercepts it looks like he does—we're talking about a suitcase nuke, or at least the makings for a very dirty bomb. Fallout covering the footprint of Manhattan."

Neil's classmate Pete is running phone traces beside us. He turns.

"We could always pull a switcheroo."

"How do you mean?" I ask.

"Swap out some little component so the thing doesn't actually work, then sell it on to al Qa'ida or JI or whatever assholes we want the most. Same thing we did with the nuclear plans and Iran."

"'Cause that turned out great," I say.

He's referring to Operation Merlin, a

botched effort from a few years back that's just been leaked to the press. In a bid to entrap the Iranians into building a nuclear weapon in contravention of the ban, we apparently arranged for an asset to pass them plans for a contraband firing mechanism, sneakily—or so we thought—adapted to render the system inoperable. As it turns out, though, Iranians are pretty good at math. Excellent, in fact. They used the correct portions of the plans, fixed the mistakes, and earned themselves a whole slew of new and useful information before we could say "underestimating the enemy." Like so many aspects of Agency history, this was unknown to any of us foot soldiers till it was published in the papers. Hard to avoid making the same mistakes twice when nobody on the inside will tell you what they were.

"Seems like the only real win here would be recruiting Jakab," I say. "Turning him to the good side. Everything else is just a delay tactic."

The guys exchange glances, like they saw that one coming. More than anyone else in the safe house, I've come to advocate for recruiting adversaries to our side rather than stealing information or material without the target's knowledge. It seems like an obvious long-term advantage to me, like winning pieces over to your side in a game of Othello.

"What is it the fortune cookies say?" I ask. "The only way to get rid of an enemy is to make him your friend?"

"Or kill him," Neil offers.

"That just creates ten more terrorists who are pissed he's dead," Pete replies. Neil shoots him some scorn.

"Hot for teacher, Petey?" Neil asks. "You're starting to sound just like her."

I pretend to miss that.

"Think about it," I say. "If we recruit him, we can work with him to reach other sellers, the ones with established client lists. Those are the big guns. As far as I can tell, Jakab doesn't have top-tier buyers yet. For all we know, he doesn't have any."

It's a big swing, recruiting rather than just buying. If we opt to buy from him, we can start right away, collect as many weapons as he's willing to sell, and take some passing comfort in the knowledge that we'll get a few nightmare machines off the street before we lose him. But if Jakab doesn't see the weapons he sells us get sold on, sooner or later he's going to get spooked. Dealers won't sell to stockpilers for long—too much risk that they're handing over evidence to Interpol or the FBI, and no savvy seller wants to hammer nails into their own potential coffin. Recruit him, on the other hand, and we can pay him to get as many weapons as possible off the market, while tapping his Rolodex for more established sellers, buying components from each, and assessing which might be susceptible to recruitment themselves. Problem is, recruitments don't happen overnight. They take time and skill and luck and patience. Any number of things can go wrong, many of which we don't control. But we can buy components from him in the meantime, and the payoff of potential recruitment down the road is worth the investment of time and attention along the way.

"Dirtbag isn't going to up and put on a superhero cape just because we give him the chance," Neil says. "And the minute we tip our hand with a recruitment pitch, we risk losing him for good."

"Not just him," my boss says from the corner. I hadn't seen him there. "A rejected recruitment pitch is gonna burn us for the entire network."

There's not a whole lot of benefit of the doubt in this safe house. "Once a schmuck, always a schmuck" is the general sentiment in most of these cubicles.

"Let's two-track it," I say. "We'll buy from him, but with a view toward eventual recruitment. That means one consistent handling officer to cement rapport, ongoing validation tests to determine his credibility, and sufficient security to be sure that if we finally do pop the question, he'll realize that he hasn't been seen in our company from the outset."

Neil and Pete look back toward our boss. He shrugs.

"So long as you're willing to walk away," he says.

"If the validation tests show up dodgy or we don't find a solid way in, some reason he'd want to work with us, then I'll drop it. Scout's honor. And we'll have been buying from him anyway, so we won't have lost anything for keeping an open mind."

Our boss looks amused. "Hard to argue with that," he says.

—

Slowly, my team learns not to bring me a proposal for buying or stealing materials if it doesn't include a plan to try turning the seller. And the more we try the two-track approach, the more successful we become. Soon, fully a quarter of the street-level dealers in the network are working with us to one degree or another, handing over the materials they buy or making introductions to other sellers higher up the chain. We haven't turned Jakab, though. After that initial meeting, I'm determined to take it slow with him.

After a good few months, I trigger a meeting via the e-mail Drafts folder and sip coffee while waiting for him on a hotel balcony off the coast of Tunisia. I've chosen this room because it looks out onto the ocean and affords no sight lines to casual observers on the shore.

He arrives singing. When I offer him a cigarette, he tells me he's quitting, then takes one anyway. This time, I wait to dive into work. Instead, we make small talk about air travel and savory pies and the ever-kitschy Eurovision Song Contest. I ask him about his signet ring, a big, gold, Super Bowl–sized affair with the figure of a lamb engraved in the center.

"It was my grandfather's," he says. "It reminds me not to go soft."

"He was a tough guy?" I ask.

"He was a lamb. And he got torn apart by the lions. This ring and an empty money clip were all they gave my mother to identify his remains."

I hold his eye for a minute. I can feel his

emotion at revisiting the memory—suddenly he is a boy again, watching his mother cry.

"Who were the lions?" I ask.

"Rákosi's pig goons," he says, and I realize he's referring to the Communist dictator I happened to have just read about in **The Economist** a few airplane flights ago. He sentenced thousands of academics to hard labor, torture, and death in midcentury Hungary, but I'd never heard of him until that article. The universe is funny that way, offering up just the facts I need a few weeks before I'll need them. "Fucking Soviets," he says. "Now I take their toys the way they took my family."

"Seems fair," I say and light a cigarette. We smoke there, side by side, for a minute, with the stucco walls on either side of us and the ocean stretching out to the horizon like a choppy Rothko in blues.

I'm determined not to broach the subject of business first. So, it seems, is he.

"What about you?" he asks. "How did you come to be in this mess?"

"Wanted to make sure every voice gets heard," I say. I've started playing a game with myself to see how long I can go without lying to a target. Withholding information is unavoidable—for their security as well as mine—but I've gotten pretty good at avoiding outright falsehoods. In part, it's just the challenge of it that appeals to me—the wordplay involved. But increasingly, I've found that it forces me to search for some shred of shareable truth instead of settling for a convenient story. Truth casts a powerful spell, cements a bond between speaker and recipient that holds us somehow, one to the other, as we wade into deeper water.

"Arm all sides to make everyone listen?" he asks, and the smoke escapes through either side of his grin. "How very Wild West."

"Just trying to right some wrongs, same as you," I say. And he laughs a deep, echoing laugh, like there are caverns inside him.

"Mother Teresa, the arms broker," he says. "Well, don't let me stand in your way. What can I do for you?"

I let the question hang there for a beat, between us and the sea. Then, without looking at him, I bite.

"Whatcha got?"

This time he answers by listing some respectable hardware. Nothing that would alert the International Atomic Energy Agency, but there are some MANPADS on the list—the portable surface-to-air missiles al Qa'ida and the Taliban have been deploying against invading attack helicopters since the Soviets turned up. He adds a few feeler items as well, materials too far up the dual-use supply chain—applicable for both civilian and military purposes—to be restricted but still valuable to those who know what they're doing. I keep an eye on the horizon while he fishes for a reaction.

First, he mentions components needed to manufacture a specialized kind of inverter, suited to powering centrifuges that need to spin fast and steady. No terror group is likely to be interested in building and maintaining cascades of centrifuges, though. That's an item sought by rogue states trying to fire up a uranium-enrichment program. Iran, North Korea—they are the centrifuge-inverter clients. The al Qa'idas and Hizb'allahs of the world are more interested in buying ready-made tactical nukes from former Soviet arsenals or acquiring enough fissile material— plutonium or highly enriched uranium—to make a crude weapon of their own.

He gets a little warmer with his last offering, a special type of beryllium useful in making reflectors that send neutrons back into an ongoing nuclear reaction to increase the bang for the buck. With a beryllium reflector in hand, a terror cell could render a bomb using dramatically less HEU—highly enriched uranium—or plutonium than they'd require without it.

I give him a quick glance to acknowledge relevance without biting too hard. He pauses, then pitches a little harder.

"I'm guessing whoever your buyers are, they don't have a hundred pounds of material sitting around." He means highly enriched uranium, and he's right—no terror group is likely to have that much fissile material on hand. Uranium occurs naturally in the ground, but it's mostly the benign uranium 238 that's hanging around down there, waiting to be mined. When you pull it up, you get a bunch of soil, with some uranium deposits mixed in. Of that, less than 1 percent is the fissile uranium 235—the kind that can sustain a nuclear chain reaction. So the process for getting from soil to bomb goes something like this: First, start mining land known to contain uranium—dirty, difficult work far off the beaten trail. Some of the best uranium deposits are deep in the Sahara Desert. Others are in the Australian outback, the wilds of Kazakhstan, and deep in Russia's interior. Once the raw material is out of the ground, it gets milled and soaked in acid to extract the uranium, which is dried into a powder known affectionately as yellowcake.

That's the first point of practical sale. We see yellowcake—real or counterfeit—on the inventory lists of sellers like Jakab the world over. The going price is about $50,000 for the amount it would take a terror cell to craft a crude dirty bomb. But that yellowcake is still less than 1 percent uranium 235. The rest is all boring old 238.

For anyone planning to make an actual nuclear weapon—to trigger and sustain a nuclear chain reaction—that yellowcake has to go through enrichment before it will pop. First, it's got to be converted into a gas known as hex—uranium hexafluoride—and injected into centrifuges that spin at twice the speed of sound. Then the laws of physics take over, pressing the heavier uranium 238 to the outside of the drum, while the lighter uranium 235 becomes concentrated on the inside. The levels of 235 get higher and higher with every spin cycle, hitting a concentration of 5 percent for civilian power generation or an ambitious 90 percent before the uranium is useful for a weapon.

This is where the rubber hits the road for most state programs. It takes thousands of precisely engineered centrifuges, arranged in cascades, a year or more to enrich enough uranium to make one nuclear bomb. Every centrifuge contains upwards of a hundred parts, each carefully engineered to keep the machine from flying apart and destroying the rest of the cascade in the process. It's no coincidence that the Swiss—known for their precision clocks—are among the world's best crafters of centrifuges. And the price tag for the equipment pretty much requires a Swiss bank account filled with zeros. For the most part, that kind of expense is the exclusive realm of nations. Some outlier groups might have those huge financial resources and years of engineering time to draw on—Aum Shinrikyo, the apocalyptic cult that choked Tokyo subway commuters with sarin gas in 1995, turned out to have nearly a billion dollars in the bank and a uranium-mining operation in Australia—but most nonstate actors are looking to skip the pesky, expensive enrichment step and purchase a ready-made weapon instead. Short of that, they're out to buy uranium that's already been concentrated so they can craft a crude weapon of their own.

It's the enrichment that takes time, skill, money. Once a group has the HEU in hand, the bomb making itself is pretty straightforward. The more HEU a group has, the easier that bomb making becomes. The hundred pounds of "material" Jakab's talking about is enough to fuel the simplest gun-style design—the same kind the United States used in Hiroshima.

But as Jakab points out, there's not much chance that any group I'd represent has a hundred pounds of highly enriched uranium burning a hole in their pocket. The less a group has, the more it needs things like the reflectors he's selling to coax along the nuclear reaction and juice the weapon's impact. Using the beryllium he's hocking, a terror cell could make something serviceable with ten pounds of plutonium. About the size of a softball, that's a much easier quantity to buy, transport, handle, and store. He's talking al Qa'ida's language, and he knows it.

"Beryllium could work," I say. "Give me the details and I'll circle back."

When we finish, Jakab heads toward the stairs to the street and I walk the other way, to the shared bathrooms at the end of the hall. I scribble notes on index cards in the toilet stall to be sure I'm able to capture everything in my summary cable to headquarters later. Each cable I write, from the moment of first contact, is copied to Jakab's file and used to assess his suitability for recruitment down the road. If I ever want the chance to actually turn him, his file has to make the strongest possible case. In coded shorthand, I list the items he offered for sale, along with price, source, and any other details he shared about each. Beneath, I write the word "Mary" to remind me of the lamb and the grandfather and Rákosi's torture goon squad. It will be an important detail come recruitment time, when I'll have to jump through a series of annoying but well-intended hoops, known as the asset validation system. AVS, as it's known, involves pointing to cables in Jakab's file that can demonstrate his sincerity, his access, and sufficient vulnerabilities to make his recruitment possible.

The word "vulnerabilities" here is a term of art, but I don't like it much. The Agency uses it to mean any need a source reveals that might make him want to work with us. Sometimes that thing truly is a vulnerability—a crushing debt or medical problem, for example. Some operatives use those inroads to get an asset on their side. I prefer a different kind of vulnerability: the desire to do something that matters. Cheesy as it sounds, I've found that deep down, most targets yearn to be a part of saving lives or bringing liberty to their lands. Like anyone else, assets want to be a part of something important, want their lives to have meant something, want to build some legacy, secret or not, to keep the terrors of mortality and insignificance at bay. That's a vulnerability all humans share. And it's the one I've found propels some of the most courageous and significant work any asset—or person—can do.

Today, Jakab wears the story of his grandfather's murder as armor to keep him hard. With some work, I'm hoping he can see it is a family legacy of opposition to fearful forces— a legacy he can honor and carry on. It can't have been easy for his grandfather to face the dreaded torture squad and hold his ideological ground. Something about the melancholy of Jakab's folk songs makes me believe that deep down, he shares his grandfather's idealism. He just needs the opportunity to surprise himself with his own ethical true north.

I tuck the index cards into the concealment pouch sewn along the inside seam of my bag. Then I return the unused cards to a leather card holder—a graduation gift from my branch chief at the Farm. In the movies, a Glock is a spy's best friend. In real life, it's the humble index card, lined on one side for meeting notes, blank on the other for hand-sketched diagrams, schematics, and maps. These three-by-five-inch rectangles of sacred information are our reason for existence. Operatives have killed and died for words written on similar cards pulled from similar holders since the days of the OSS. And those words have saved countless lives, averting nuclear disaster and preventing imminent attacks from Pyongyang to Havana.

14

When I get back to the Virginia safe house, I lay out the meeting cards on my desk. Jakab had mentioned that he had a few contacts who used to work at Arzamas-16, one of the most advanced of the former Soviet nuclear labs. That goes some way to corroborating Neil's conference room map and its tentacle connections between Jakab and a smorgasbord of dealers offering the highest-end nuclear goods. It also suggests that he hasn't given me his full catalog just yet. Beryllium reflectors and precision inverters are all well and good, but Arzamas-16 is a full-on Aladdin's cave of destruction. Anyone with the kind of access he described should be able to get their hands on the holy grail of nuclear terrorism: the much-sought-after, man-portable, airline-checkable suitcase nuke.

Only one-fifteenth as strong as either of the atomic bombs dropped on Hiroshima, this tactical weapon would still claim a few hundred thousand lives over a few decades and render an entire city center uninhabitable. These bombs require no codes to operate, and at the very least, we believe that 150 to 200 of them are missing from the former Soviet arsenal. Arzamas-16 was a storage site for suitcase nukes back when the Soviet Union fell and the security layer accountable for tracking its weapons fell right along with it. Many were stashed in rooms secured only with padlocks—the kind that can be dispatched with a pair of garden-variety bolt cutters. Across the former Soviet empire, labs like Arzamas-16 were overrun by confusion and economic hardship. Chains of command crumbled, and entire swaths of the Soviet military complex devolved to every man for himself. Potatoes were better guarded than nuclear weapons. Until workers realized that a bomb can buy a lot of potatoes. And by then, it was too late.

"Technically, he's our lowest-level dealer," Neil says on reviewing my notes. "Given that you seem to be his best customer just now. But in terms of connections, he might be one of our best."

I nod. There's something special about Jakab—that elusive mix of honor and access that gets my adrenaline racing. Sure, he's not making the most righteous choices at the moment, but the potential is there. I can taste it.

"He's ours to lose," I say.

"Let him cool his heels," Neil agrees. "Then draft an e-mail ordering the right amount of beryllium for a coy little reflector. Should be enough to whet his appetite."

It's a rush, juggling communications with every dealer in the network, keeping straight where each is in our recruitment process, what materials each sells, and, most important, what drives them to sell materials at all. In addition to Jakab, I'm working three others. Neil and Pete have two each. Between us, we have another half dozen in the early throes of e-mail inquiry. And that's just the brokers. We're also each handling existing assets in the terror groups themselves in order to find out where they're sourcing their weapons and add those nodes to the network we're mapping.

It's a different feeling, meeting a source who was recruited by a previous operative. There isn't a shared history to draw on, except for whatever the handling officer captured in his or her cables. I pore over each asset's file before I meet them, memorizing the visual and spoken cues we'll need to exchange to confirm each other's identity and reviewing their personal histories, searching out every last hint about what makes this person tick. All CIA assets put themselves at risk by working with us, but none more so than these sources, nestled deep inside terror groups that exist to see us dead. Many do it only as a last resort, an ethical emergency-stop button they hit when the plans of their brothers become one step too extreme. Even so, it's never easy. In many cases, we are still their enemy, and understanding the nuances of their motivation is critical to getting out of each meeting alive.

One of them—an Egyptian named Karim—triggers a meeting a month or so after I get back from Tunisia. His file says he was a walk-in, a source who turned up at the embassy in Amman one day, asking to talk with the CIA. I cringe thinking about the poor officer on duty. Some walk-ins provide our very best information. Other walk-ins are dangles—bait sent by a terror group or hostile intelligence service to sniff out which embassy staffers are actually CIA. That means the operative assigned to take the meeting has to kit up in light disguise—the wig, glasses, and latex nose debacle issued by the DS&T and better suited to a **Saturday Night Live** skit than a life-or-death chat with a sworn enemy. I only hope that whoever took this particular walk-in didn't have hair as long as mine, because the cable says the meeting lasted four and a half hours, and those wigs begin to ride up around the end of hour one.

When he walked into the embassy, Karim came armed with nothing—no weapons, no documents, no photos to prove what he had to say. Only a wild story of his al Qa'ida cell's search for nuclear weapons in the backcountry of Chechnya. Methodically, the embassy officer debriefed him, asking him to draw bird's-eye-view diagrams of each compound or village he mentioned. When compared to satellite imagery, every diagram checked out. He'd been recruited as a low-level courier by an al Qa'ida cell when his parents died. He'd needed a way to feed himself and his little brother. The more responsibility they gave him, the more trapped he became. Until one day, they asked him to meet with a broker about a bomb. He hated us, he clarified that first day. Hated us enough not to become like us. Only the Great Satan deploys nuclear weapons, he told the walk-in officer. Karim went on to become one of our most valuable sources in mapping al Qa'ida's search for nuclear technology. He is a treasure of national security. But his handling officer quit the Agency unexpectedly last month, so when Karim signals for a meeting, I'm the one who gets on a plane.

According to the commo plan on file, we're to meet in the private courtyard of a rented apartment in Erbil, an ancient city in northern Iraq. The war is quieter up here, beyond the moonscape of Anbar. There are still suicide bombings, like the one that killed upwards of fifty people in May, but the local Kurdish militia keeps snipers off the streets. Karim's been living outside Mosul this last year, half a day's car ride away, counting the time spent stuck behind oil trucks or facedown at check-points. He comes into Erbil periodically for meetings and supplies.

There's something about Iraq that strikes my tuning fork. About the whole Middle East, really. The street music, the smell of hummus and lamb, the tradition of hospital-ity, even from those who have nothing. There is an ancient knowing here, beneath all the blood sport and fear.

I meander through the **souq** during the last phase of my surveillance detection route. It's said to be the oldest continuously operating marketplace in the world, going back some seven thousand years. Dazzling **suzanis** are piled to the ceiling, their hand embroidery like Technicolor spiderwebs against the dusty walls. Peddlers sell remote-controlled toys and beeping plastic robots. Clothing stalls display knock-off Nikes alongside bedazzled hijabs. An assortment of religious jewelry catches my eye. Amid prayer beads and **ayatul kursi** scrolls, a small selection of pendants includes a coin that reads "You shall know the truth and the truth shall make you free." They're the same words that are etched on the wall of the Agency atrium, across from the rows of stars that represent the sacrifice of generations of spies. Funny to see Christian scripture here, in this Muslim land. I wonder how many Americans, how many Iraqis, remember that Jesus is considered a prophet in Islam.

"How much?" I ask the bent man behind the table, and, after exchanging a few notes, tuck the coin in my pocket as I continue on toward my meeting.

I find a coffeehouse a little ways down a cobbled road and take a seat, my final timing stop, designed to allow me to approach my meeting place within the specified four-minute window. An old Kurdish woman offers to read my coffee grounds. I ignore her, then tell her thanks but no. She stands there, plump and sincere, as I take my last sip and pack away the drinks and pastries I've bought for the meeting. I glance at my watch. Still a few minutes until it makes sense to leave. I've already determined that I'm not under surveillance. Might as well consult with the spirits.

I turn my cup over on the saucer and look up at her. She motions for me to hand it to her as she takes the seat across from me. The road beside us is filled with bicycles. She lifts up my cup and peers at the shapes in the grainy black grounds.

"A bird!" she exclaims. "Here, look. A bird with"—she flicks her hand like Wolverine— "claws."

She's pointing to a shape in the center of the saucer. It does, in truth, look exactly like a bird with claws.

"Birds mean the bringing of a message. It is a happy thing. Claw means an enemy. It is a frightening thing." It feels implausible that my coffee grounds could summarize my upcoming meeting so accurately. For a moment, I wonder if she's Kurdish intelligence. Then she puts her hand on mine, as though she is giving me a gift. "And here," she says, "is a broom and a butterfly." She points to the shapes with her pinkie. It's inexplicably endearing, this old crone making such an effort to be delicate with her cracked and swollen fingers. "The broom is for questioning what you think you know. And the butterfly is for"—she passes her hands quickly in front of her heart like curtains—"transformation. It is a very lucky reading," she says. I give her five thousand dinars and stand up. She holds my eye. "Very lucky," she repeats as I go.

They're generic things, I tell myself. Could apply to anyone. Still, her sincerity stays with me as I make the last few turns before the meeting. What would I hope to transform into, I find myself wondering, if that butterfly were me. Someone who doesn't transform for a living, maybe. Someone who gets to just be.

I enter the apartment building's lobby. It's sparse but clean. The commo plan says to meet in Flat 5. I let myself in and dead-bolt the door behind myself. A pair of shutters opens to the little courtyard, set with a table and chairs beside a small tile fountain. A pair of doors leads to the street. I unlock them and roll an empty oil drum out onto the pavement—the specified signal to indicate that all is safe for Karim to enter. A few minutes later, he does.

He is slender and taut, the skin pulled tightly over his cheekbones. I lock the street door behind him. When I turn back to him, I notice that his eyes are green.

"What brings you to Erbil?" I ask him, the opening of oral bona fides, an exchange of predesignated sentences to confirm each other's identities.

"The call of the mufti," he replies. Most assets recite their bona fides with boredom or irritation, but he says the words with exquisite feeling, as though they are not only true but urgent.

"Thanks for coming," I say and gesture for him to take a seat. I pull out the drinks and pastries and join him at the table. He watches me but says nothing. His breath is slower than mine.

"Did you run into any problems on the way?"

He offers a slight head shake, no more than a twitch.

"Great. And how much time do we have to chat?"

He glances at his phone. "Five minutes," he says.

I hold my hand out toward the handset. "May I?" I ask. He clicks the battery out himself and lays it on the table. "Thanks," I say and lay my watch on the table. "Sounds like we need to be quick. If anyone interrupts us, we're here because you want to buy some art." I pull a pile of art magazines out of my backpack and scatter them around us. It's a flimsy cover, likely to fall apart the moment he and I are questioned separately, but with only five minutes for the meeting, it's all the time I can spare. I become still and look into his eyes.

"Why did you trigger the meeting?" I ask.

"My Chechen hookup went dark," he says, and from the previous meeting notes, I know that he means the broker he was tasked to approach for a chunk of uranium. "Might have gotten himself wrapped up, I don't know. Or killed. My commander wants me to find someone new."

It's a hell of an opportunity, getting to direct al Qa'ida's choice of nuclear arms dealer. One that's going to require some consultation with HQS.

"I'd like to get some input from my people here," I say. "Can we meet again in a few days? How long do you have to decide on a name?"

"Five minutes," he repeats, holding my eye. I search his gaze for a beat. He looks frightened inside there, somewhere under the calm demeanor.

"Are you being followed?" I ask him.

"Not right now. But I'm traveling with

someone. He watches me. I could only get away for a second. If I don't have a name when I get back, I'll get pulled off this task. They're blaming me for the Chechen dead end." His green eyes look at mine with pleading. "I tried, okay? If you hadn't blown up Hiroshima, they wouldn't be looking for these things to begin with. Just let me leave them, okay? I just want to move on with my life."

Karim is one of only a handful of sources with access to al Qa'ida's nuclear aspirations. Losing him would be a devastating blow. There's no time to consult with HQS. I roll the dice.

"All right, look, I'm going to introduce you to a Hungarian named Jakab. Draw out the introductory conversations as long as you can."

"He's credible?" Karim asks. In his voice I hear the subtext: Can I bet my life on using his name?

"He's credible," I say.

"But you're going to stop him from actually selling them anything," he says.

"Karim, you told us you couldn't bear the idea of stooping as low as Saddam. In his case, it was chemical weapons. In this case, it would be what? A suitcase nuke? Women

and children. Young people. Your brother."
He looks as though he might cry.

I write an e-mail address and password on
an index card. It's a crapshoot—an account
I haven't yet set up. For all I know, the
username is taken. But I can't compromise
an existing account, so there's nothing for it
but to take the chance. Birdclawbroomfly@
hotmail.com.

"Log in and check the Drafts folder. I'll
have left you a message of introduction to
Jakab there. You can correspond with him
the same way."

He takes it from me, his eyes still on
mine. They are impossibly sorrowful, like a
Miyazaki character's, searching for someone
to trust.

"You're a good brother," I tell him. "And
a good man. We'll find a way through this."

He nods, as though he doesn't quite have
the confidence to speak without crying.

"You're doing the right thing, Karim."

—

When I get back to the Virginia safe house,
it's happy hour. My boss pours me a whiskey.
"Holy hell, if he'd have quit, we'd be

explaining ourselves on the seventh floor," he says, referring to the level at HQS where senior leadership sits. "You did good this time." He raises a glass. "To the schmuck whisperer," he says, and the name sticks like glue.

They're not wrong. Many of our sources are schmucks—brokers and fighters looking to sell death or deliver it. But some reserved corner of their secret selves is still human, too. And it's a good operative's job to find it. Speak to that hidden humanity and you've got yourself an ally. That's the theory, anyway.

And it seems to be working. Jakab appreciates the introduction, and Karim stretches it out as long as possible. It earns me credibility with both of them. But it's a dangerous game, playing against the ticking clock of an actual sale. And it's one we're playing on multiple boards simultaneously, recruiting brokers and fighters across three continents as we move slowly up the traffickers' ranks.

On my rare trips into HQS, I can't tell anyone I see in the halls where the safe house is or what kind of operations we run from it. Even Dean thinks I'm in language training for an eventual move to a base in China, though he knows not to ask too many questions about my nonprogressing ability to order Chinese takeout every time he's home.

It's not always easy, keeping secrets from spies. One middle manager corners me after a briefing at HQS and asks for driving directions to our safe house. When I explain that he'll need to apply for access, he tells me how high his clearance is. Tells me how many tours he's done. How many awards he has. How high his pay grade is. Everything short of how much he can bench-press. None of which exempts him from the requirement to apply. But the fact that I, a woman—a girl—have information he cannot demand from me seems to infuriate him. He tells me to drive him to the safe house or risk being fired. I drive him to the administrative building where he can file his application for access instead. When I pull into the parking lot, he gets out of the car and spits on the ground.

"You better hope you don't get reported," he says. I freeze up. Complying with the security procedures was the right thing to do, I know, but he has power in this world and I don't.

"I'm just trying to follow the rules," I say.

"Would be a shame if someone filed a complaint. Sexual harassment maybe," he says and smiles. For days after that, my pulse still quickens each time I check my e-mail. Suppose he makes good on his threat and manufactures some offense. What the hell would I say?

Being a woman at the Agency is to belong to a small club—a club whose members don't yet eat often in the exclusive seventh-floor dining room, reserved for senior leadership, or kick back after work at the gentlemen's clubs that pepper McLean. There are a few female managers I think would believe me, having experienced the same pressure to bend the rules for male bosses. But they themselves are mostly outranked by members of the old boys' club who've served together in the camaraderie of the Cold War days. All that machismo is destined to change. Not two decades hence, the unique skill set women bring to this work—the emotional intelligence, aptitude for multitasking, and keen intuition that make women such exceptional operatives—will propel female officers to the highest roles of leadership across the organization. But in that parking lot on that lonely afternoon, women don't yet have the power to protect their own. And I fear for my job.

A week or so later, my chief calls me into his office. I wait for the slap in the face, prepare myself to hear whatever outrageous claim has been made to punish me for standing up to a man accustomed to making rules bend to his will. But instead, my boss tells me our operation is working, and we need to shift into higher gear. The dealers think my art business is cover for a weapons brokerage. As we move higher up the ladder, we need to be sure that the brokerage doesn't have any American fingerprints on it. We want as distant a home base as possible, to offset any attention our success might bring our way and create plenty of blue water between the business I'm using to run this operation and the Stars and Stripes, which funds it. In short, he's moving me to Shanghai.

My relief at not being fired is immediately drowned out by a flood of adrenaline. Moving this program overseas is a big step—a vote of confidence and an upshift in the level of danger. I'm determined to rise to the task.

My cover will be establishing an Asian office for the business, he tells me, focused on emerging artists throughout the Middle East. Up until now, my fictional career in tribal artwork has been for the benefit of customs agents on my brief trips overseas and my family and friends back home. Neither ever spent more than twenty minutes asking me questions about it. Once in China, it will be a twenty-four/seven fiction, requiring as much time and attention as a real business, but I'll need to make space for my operational work, too. I go through a one-week crash-course MBA, designed to make sure I know my balance sheet from my cap table, should I be questioned by foreign authorities. I receive express instructions not to conduct any part of any operation in China itself. It's to be a home base only, though I'm told to expect near-constant surveillance nonetheless.

All actual operational activity will happen in other countries, mostly under my true name but sometimes under an alias, which means flying to a different country, swapping out my documents, and continuing to the operational destination with my fictional identity in hand. The point of nonofficial cover is to keep the stench of officialdom at bay, so doc swaps can't be undertaken in embassies. Instead, we rely mostly on the brush pass, a piece of tradecraft that involves timing a stroll to intersect with another operative's path in a predesignated location—a tunnel or alleyway, somewhere secluded enough that no trailing surveillance has the chance to see documents exchanged between us as we pass without breaking stride.

Brush passes require a fair bit of planning, with both operatives conducting surveillance detection routes on their way to the act. Once I have my new alias docs in hand, there's the matter of memorizing my new identity before getting back to the airport, an activity usually undertaken in a bathroom stall, and the sprinkling of the included pocket litter through my backpack and luggage: grocery store receipts and birthday cards to reinforce the cover. All that hassle means that working in alias isn't the most efficient way to tackle a meeting, but it can be the most effective, especially when identities need to be protected—when the destination government is an adversary or we need to keep a firewall between one asset and another. The chief instructs me to pick up an extra set of alias docs before I leave, in case I have to travel incognito without time to arrange a swap.

Finally, he tells me that Dean and I face a choice. I either deploy alone and we're forbidden to have contact for the six years I'll be overseas. Or it's another administrative marriage. We can move to China together, but only if we tie the knot before we leave.

When we're on R&R in Hawaii, I prepare myself to talk with Dean about this, but he beats me to it with a ring on a windswept bluff underneath the mural of a sea turtle. "Your boss talk to you, too?" I ask him, and he kisses me.

"Six years apart or a lifetime together—not much of a quandary," he says. We've never even uttered the word "love" to each other. Never lived in the same city. Never met each other's families. It's a proposal made of practicality, and it's out of practicality that I accept. He's the most talented officer I know. Six years is a long time to work alone. We both know that. And in knowing that we both know it, we are happy. Our little circle of pragmatic honesty in the midst of a swirl of fiction.

15

That night, I watch his eyes dart behind closed lids as he sleeps. I wish I could see what he's seeing, wish I could experience his memories, his fears, his flashbacks, his dreams. But he's as opaque to me as I am to him. He wouldn't recognize my soul, I know, if he met it outside my body. He couldn't identify my memories of Laura's laugh or Danny's grace. Wouldn't understand my hunger to memorialize them by finding some way forward.

"You can't exactly end the war from inside the war machine," he'd said, laughing, in the gazebo when we first met.

"What if that's the only place you can end it?" I asked him. And in changing the subject, he sealed off from himself a part of me that couldn't be reopened.

Still, spies are no stranger to locked com-

partments, and we've found a mutual respect in the areas that remain. It's okay that
he doesn't know how much the lies that come
with our work are beginning to bother me,
how I'm starting to have trouble shedding my
cover even when I'm alone. I've been pretending to be an arms dealer pretending to be an
art dealer for over a year now, and it's harder
to tell which part of me is her and which part
of me is me. Would I be able to make the
same impact if I lived life in my true skin?

Dean startles in his sleep, and I know he'd
tell my mind to hush if he could hear it.
Maybe he's right. It's no time to contemplate
peeling off the armor just as we're about to
wade deeper into war. The ring he gave me
hangs loose on my finger, like a life preserver
or a shackle. Either way, it will keep me tied
to my moorings. And that's better than the
void just now.

We get married two days before Dean's
birthday, alone on a beach in Zanzibar. At
twenty-seven years old, I look at him as the
local priest holds our hands together on a
bleached white strip of sand and explains the
seriousness of what we are doing. I realize
then that I don't know Dean at all. But it's
a leap of faith. And at that point, though he
doesn't know me either, he's just about the

closest thing there is to someone who does. He's been through the same training, the same bureaucratic labyrinth of unjustified lies wrapped up in justified ones. He knows some, not all, of my factual secrets, even if he doesn't know any of my spiritual ones. And somehow that feels good enough.

The next morning, we fight. I can't remember what about. And I sit next to him beside a swimming pool, in the sudden, isolated silence, feeling the years of not knowing each other stretching out ahead, wondering if it might have been less lonely to deploy alone after all.

The day after that is his birthday, and I blow up balloons during the night so the hotel room will be full of them when he wakes. I want to make him smile, erase the fearful what-have-we-done's of the day before. But instead the balloons startle him when he steps on one in the dark, and the squeal sets off memories of somewhere unsafe, then anger at having been made to remember.

By the time we leave Zanzibar, a kind of muted pragmatism has set in, fueled by mutual respect and the unspoken sense that mission trumps emotion. We're on track to finish our separate tours of duty and deploy together the next month. There's no reversing course.

On the way to the airport, as our hotel van winds its way through the predawn jungle roads, a truck suddenly screams past us and turns sharply to cut us off. It's a classic ambush move, and Tanzania is a tinderbox just then. We exchange looks, ready to get the hell off the X. Dean uses his eyes to propose an exit strategy. I nod, almost imperceptibly. Our bodies flood with adrenaline. The man in the truck jumps out, runs toward the van, throws something at the driver. The driver grins back at us. "Forgot this," he says, holding up his cell phone. We exhale. Dean gives my hand a squeeze. In that moment, I know he has my back. And it occurs to me, as we pick up speed through the jungle, that having each other's backs is pretty much all we can ask of ourselves just then.

—

When we get back to work, the chief swings by my desk.

"Congratulations," he says, with a nod at my ring. "You married the Agency." I give him a half-smile. He's not wrong. "Now take my advice and start pretending you mean it. This whole thing's going to be a lot easier on you if you start accepting you're in it for life."

I think about his words that afternoon as I line up downtown to pick up my alias passport.

Our operational docs are issued by the real DMV or passport authority or Social Security Administration, unflagged to almost anyone in those offices, save a highly cleared liaison officer who slips our applications through the system unchecked. Perfectly authentic documents mean less chance of ending up in a foreign prison. They also mean more hours in DMV-style waiting rooms, listening to numbers gets called while **Judge Judy** plays on mute.

I sit in a hard plastic chair and replay the chief's words in my head. **Accept that you're in it for life.** That's what he said. It sounds obvious, clichéd, even, like fortune cookie wisdom, but the more I think about it, the more compelling it becomes. Maybe living a lie hurts only so long as I keep reminding myself it's a lie. Maybe if I just act like it's real, believe it's real, even when I'm alone, maybe someday the longing for life without cover will disappear and my shell will just become my skin.

"Let's go all in," I tell Dean when he gets back from Afghanistan for the last time. And together, we decide to throw away the Pill.

We rent a little house on a leafy road in northern Virginia. It's old and creaky, with two tiny bedrooms side by side—ours on the left and an empty one on the right. We'll have moved overseas before any baby could possibly come, but the doorway of that room smiles at me every time I walk up the stairs.

Out back, there's a scraggly field, full of bumps and bare patches and scattered wildflowers. We sit there some nights, on the wooden back steps, drinking wine and watching the lightning bugs blink their way across the dusk. One time, we see a bat swoop down from under the eaves.

"Think he lives with us?" I ask.

"Just freak out about it," Dean says.

"I can handle al Qa'ida. Pretty sure I can handle a bat," I answer. "Why, you squeamish?"

"My mom used to be. One got stuck in our living room when I was a kid. Fluttering and flying all over the place. Mom was screaming at my dad to get it out, but the ceiling was too high and he couldn't reach it. He went straight out to the garage and came back with a tennis racket and a screwdriver. Pinned the bat against the wall with the racket and stabbed it to death with the screwdriver, right above the fireplace. Blood splatter was there the whole rest of my childhood. And every time I looked at it, I thought, 'That's my dad. That's a real man. That's how a man protects his castle,' you know?"

I can't tell if it's supposed to be a happy memory. I want to hug him. Want to tell him I'm sorry he saw that. But he's smiling and pouring more wine, like the story is a fond one.

"Did your dad ever talk about the war?" I ask. He looks at me curiously, as if it's a non sequitur.

"Vietnam?" he asks. "Not really. It fucked him up. He doesn't mention it much."

I think of the room directly beneath us, the basement Dean's turned into his man cave, its walls lined with combat gear he no longer needs.

"It can be addictive, though," I say.

"You're saying he took it out on the bat?" Dean asks. It's an air ball—one of those moments that could turn into a fight. We sit there for a beat, charged with defensiveness and worry. Then he softens. Presses the hair off my face and kisses me. I'm glad for the escape. It lurks in the back of my mind, though, the specter of trauma handed down from father to son. Were they so different, Vietnam and Afghanistan? What bats will Dean one day need to kill?

"You're a loon, you know that?" he asks, and before I can think anymore, we find our way naked to bed.

The month before we deploy, I go with my mom to CarMax to sell my car. We're squeezing every last second out of our time together, best friends clinging to a phase of life we know will never return. Sitting at the plastic table in the waiting area, beside the vending machines, I pull out a pregnancy test to show her. Two pink lines that will become a person eight months hence. I've thought a hundred times about the day my mom and I would get to share this news, but never, in all those times, did I dream it would be in a CarMax waiting room on my way to live undercover in China. My mom looks at me wistfully. "Can't you work with American artists?"

"Have to break down the barriers," I say. "Share foreign points of view."

"Can't you do that from here?" she asks.

"Someday," I say. And catch myself praying it's true.

—

Dean and I arrive in Shanghai in the windswept cold of January. There are to be no trips home at first, no connection with the States at all. Plucked free of all remaining moorings, I have a harder and harder time remembering which part of me is real.

An actor friend of mine likes to tell this story. It starts with him agreeing to play a homeless heroin addict on the streets of L.A. He's a Daniel Day-Lewis type, so a month before they start filming, he sets out to immerse himself in the role. First, he locks his apartment door and gives the key to his girlfriend. Then he catches a bus to skid row. And then he buys some smack.

When his girlfriend comes to find him thirty days later, he's living under a tarp pinned between a dumpster and a wall. He's lost fifteen pounds. He's gained a tattoo. He kicks the air as she approaches. "C'mon, sweets," she says. "You start shooting on Monday."

At this point in the telling, my friend likes to roll up his sleeve, pat the inside of his forearm, and say, "So I tell her I'm already shooting." Wry smile. "And she gets right in my face. She looks me in the eyes. And she says, 'Jake, you're an actor. You're researching a part.' And I look right back at her and say, 'I am?'"

Pretending is like that. The better you get at it, the more you forget you're doing it. Until one day you wake up behind a dumpster.

Or in my case, in a Chinese hotel room, staring at the smoke detector's blinking red light in the dark.

I'm pretty good at pretending by this point. Professional, even. But I've always had breaks—time back in D.C. between trips, time in the safe house with Jon and Neil and Pete, time at the pub with Mike and Dave— a makeshift family of others who share my dual reality. This is my first time living the lie around the clock. The years of deception yawn ahead, like an ink-black void. No moments of respite, no footholds from which to touch the truth. Just us and our covcom and our fictions, layer upon layer of lies.

We're staying in a hotel in Shanghai while we look for a permanent house. Langley has told us to assume that the room is wired for surveillance, audio and visual, night vision and all.

My husband is asleep beside me, his breathing still not totally familiar. Our baby is beginning to uncurl beneath my navel.

Maybe it's the jet lag. Or the pregnancy hormones. Or the idea of a roomful of strangers gawking at our naked bodies somewhere outside Beijing. But no matter how many blinking lights I count, I can't fall asleep.

The stillness is getting to me, smothering me with its false sense of security. **Nothing to** worry about, Amaryllis. Just them watching us watching them. The spy game. The natural way of things. Go to sleep.

Blink, one, two, three, blink.

Go to sleep.

Until finally I give up and climb out of bed, slide open the bathroom door, and flip on the light. Everything is as it should be. Sink, mirror, flower in its little blown-glass vase. The contemporary design of anonymous business hotels everywhere. And yet, from behind pinhole and fixture, they're watching.

"Just pretend to be yourself," Langley has taught us, apparently without irony.

I pee. Wash my hands. Make a face at myself in the mirror. Silently ask myself after each beat, "What would I do next? If I were really me?" I've asked myself that question in other hotel rooms in other countries. But it's here, in this Chinese bathroom at dawn, that I realize I don't know the answer.

It's startling, like being passed a note from my waking self to alert me that I'm actually in the midst of a dream.

Suddenly, the sink and the mirror and the blown-glass vase seem like nothing more than a stage scrim—realistic enough, but transient and cartoonish, the way I imagine things look on the holodeck of the starship **Enterprise**, ready to collapse back into their flexible atomic superstate at the touch of a button, like so much cosmic Silly Putty. I stare at my hands, resting on the cold marble swirl. Even they are something slightly less than real. I'm overwhelmed with the sudden and unsettling understanding that I'm neck-deep in a game of make-believe. And the game is so convincing, I have no idea when it began. Or who the "I" is that's playing it.

My brain sparks with an almost assaultive sensation of homecoming. Then plunges into a flooding, liquid-amber calm that feels so otherworldly, I exhale this slow Lamaze-type breath, because I don't want to get chucked back out of the wormhole.

I stare at the back of one hand and know somehow that if I move it, move even a finger, I'll melt back into the game. I stay there for a spell—a gently gawking tourist in a place both alien and familiar, like the first time I visited Shwedagon Pagoda or sat on my grandmother's grave. But camera-ridden hotel rooms in China are no place for self-inquiry. So I move my hand. And turn off the light.

I walk back across the muted carpet. Climb back into the beige bed. Close my eyes and ask myself, in the clingy, sterile quiet, when exactly it was I started pretending, so I can work forward from there, like using Version History in Google Docs.

I expect my brain to answer with memories of CIA training, my first packet of alias docs, maybe, or the first time I was trained to take a polygraph pretending to be someone I wasn't. But my waking self passes me one more note that night, in the form of a memory far older than any of those. One of those memories is so deeply packed away that I have to unfold its sepia edges gently, in case they turn to dust in my hands.

I was three, maybe, and sitting in a wooden high chair with my back to the window in our kitchen in Washington, D.C. My mom was upset. I don't remember what about. But she was magical and fierce. Like a character from **D'Aulaires' Book of Greek Myths.** The beating heart of our clan, she was the source of love and tenderness and poetry in our world. And like all poets' hearts, she felt life deeply, radiating joy and despair, often in the same afternoon.

I was afraid of her sadness the way other kids were afraid of thunder. Threatening not because it caused actual damage—my mom always returned to her sunny disposition— but because it seemed otherworldly, this strange, percussive force that arrived without warning to tear the sky in two.

Ben was at the kitchen table beside me. Our hermit crabs, Freddie and Laura, were hiding out in their terrarium on the counter. Mom was scrubbing the clean sink with a clenched sponge, like if she just applied enough elbow grease, she might be able to dissolve something painful only she could see.

Then suddenly she stopped.

Her face went calm. She set about stirring the saucepan on the stove, as though she hadn't a care in the world.

I must have imagined it, I thought. Then her eyes went to the window behind me and her smile crumbled. She dropped the spoon back in the pot, and faster than it had evaporated, her sadness returned.

A bunch of pedestrians had walked by on the brick sidewalk outside. Mom's recovery, her smile and pot stirring, had been for them—strolling strangers, peering in on our world from beyond.

For them, she'd been exactly what she thought they wanted her to be. A Stepford wife, immune to frustration and fear and pain. For us, she'd returned to what she was. A beautiful, sparkling human, experiencing the full range of that brilliant, agonizing condition.

It is, I think, my earliest memory. And the first time I understood the difference between the way we were and the way grown-ups wanted other people to think we were.

I didn't know then that twenty years later, I'd be pretending to be someone else for a living, pretending to be someone else for my country. Didn't know I'd be reliving the moment from a hotel room bed in Shanghai. Nor that one day, not too many years hence, my mother would write me a letter that would help me answer the same questions she had so many years ago set me to asking. That in loving me enough to share her lessons, she would save me.

The hotel heater kicks on and my jet lag kicks in. **Enough questions for one night,** I tell myself, and beneath the blinking light, I surrender to sleep.

16

The next morning, we meet our real estate agent on the Bund, the walkway along the river that splits Shanghai in two. On one side of the water, the ancient temples of Chinese yesteryear line the cobbled streets of the French concession. On the other side, a seemingly science fiction vision of tomorrow rises in brushed chrome and glass, dotted with sky needles and suspended bulbous orbs.

"Look," she says, after the mandatory exchange of greetings and pleasantries. "It's always the same. The foreigners are gazing at the historic buildings, looking backward, toward the past. But the Chinese tourists, the ones who come from the villages to see Shanghai for the first time, they are always gazing across the river, with their eyes on the future." It seems like a poetic oversimplification, but a quick glance up and down the Bund confirms it's true. Westerners are snapping pictures of crumbling antique roofs. Between them, a Chinese family stands very still, everyone's hands plunged in their pockets against the cold, gazing at the skyscrapers across the way. There is pride in their faces, as the wind comes off the water, like pioneers in sight of the promised land.

"Which side are you looking to live on?" the real estate agent asks.

"Hate to be clichéd," Dean says, "but we're suckers for history."

She smiles at the quaintness. "Well, we'd better get a move on. Most of the old lane houses are scheduled for destruction in the next ten years. Let's get you one while we still can!"

We settle on a ramshackle, beautiful redbrick affair, filled with an assortment of wooden opium beds and carved chests. It's a journey through China's past, a trove of antiques stashed here by a local businessman who hit it big and upgraded to right angles and reflective steel. There is a magic to this little house, a musty tomb of centuries past. And it's cheap, which earns us a few goodwill points back at Langley.

—

Like Russia, China is a hard-target country, meaning it uses the most aggressive, sophisticated counterespionage tactics in the world. We're not planning to conduct any operations in-country, but Chinese intelligence doesn't know that, and its agents make it clear that they plan to find out. From the moment we step foot on the ground, our every move is watched. It's subtle at first. China loves its static surveillance—street sellers who get paid to jot down the time whenever a foreigner comes or goes. They're a lot harder to detect than surveillance teams that move with a target across time and distance. But soon their reaching for pencil and notebook each time we pass becomes as noticeable as the eyes of forest creatures on an evening hike. When I leave a pashmina shawl in a taxi, it's returned to my front door by a policeman in uniform, despite our having paid for the ride in cash and not having told the driver our address.

"You should take care to keep track of your things," the policeman says as he stoops beneath a string of our neighbor's dried fish.

"Why bother when you do such a good job keeping track of them for us?" Dean asks from over my shoulder. I cringe. So much for keeping a polite, nonalerting profile.

"Thank you, Officer," I say and press the door closed. I lock it, as though that actually means anything. Then walk back into the living room we've been told is probably bugged.

The only way to handle being watched is to give the watchers nothing to see. We set about creating a normal-looking home for two young art dealers, Dean having been assigned to share my cover, so that we're running a family business. We sign up for language classes and start going to art world parties. We begin to make a name for ourselves, even if Dean looks a bit out of place, with his massive shoulders and military posture. There are operations I'm asked to undertake that Dean doesn't know about. I presume there are operations he is asked to undertake that I don't know about. We don't talk about work. We don't talk about anything of importance, briefed as we have been that our house is under surveillance, that even our housekeeper, a wraithlike presence named Ayi, works for Beijing, that we should have sex regularly but not too regularly, keep it hot but not too hot, that we should live our private life with the twenty-four/seven knowledge that its purpose is to give those watching the distinct impression that we don't know anyone is watching.

Operational orders arrive by way of our covcom—questions headquarters wants us to ask existing assets, traces our desk officers have run on sources we might recruit, approvals for the plans we file in advance of each third-country meeting. A few months in, I send a cable to say that I'm ready to pull the trigger on Jakab's recruitment. He's written to tell me that he plans to be in Thailand the following week, on his way to Indonesia. I've felt for a while now that he's on the brink of being ready to work with us. Ideally, I'd like to give it a few more meetings before I lay everything on the table, but Indonesia is the stomping ground of Jemaah Islamiyah, al Qa'ida's arm in Southeast Asia and the group behind the Bali nightclub bombings that stole the lives of two hundred people as they enjoyed an evening out. With a suitcase nuke or a chunk of HEU in their hands, there's no telling what JI's jihadists might do. I can't risk waiting until the timing is perfect, maybe missing the opportunity to stop a weapon from changing hands. Headquarters approves and suggests that Dean and I travel together under the guise of a babymoon.

"Why not," Dean replies when I ask him.

"Maybe we'll catch a full-moon party." The island Jakab's visiting is famous for all-night beach raves on the brightest night of each month.

"I might have to duck out for a minute," I tell him and he nods, knowing not to ask.

—

We arrive in Bangkok and board a puddle jumper to the island of Ko Tao. We're operational, I know. I'm here in-country to meet a would-be asset for a clandestine recruitment pitch. But still I vibrate a little with girlish pleasure as I take Dean's hand for our landing. Outside the window stretch beaches of white sand and milky green sea. After the dinge of Shanghai, it's lush and inviting, all freshness and possibility. It occurs to me that we might be able to reset here, snap out of the mutually imposed silence that's sucked the air from the last few months. Get to know each other in the raw, the way a married couple should, the way nobody living in a wired house ever could.

I'm due to meet Jakab a few hours after we land. "See you at the hotel?" I ask Dean as we emerge blinking into the Ko Tao sunset.

He puts an arm around me as we walk across the runway, toward the thatched roof that serves as baggage claim.

"Can't imagine you could get in too much trouble here," he says, surveying the palm trees. "But be careful anyway."

"Promise," I say and flag down a cab.

I've booked a suite at a separate hotel so that Jakab and I will have a private place to talk. Recruitment conversations are best had far away from curious passersby. Ideally, the potential source knows what is coming and is ready for it, somewhere deep down. "Think of it like a marriage proposal," my boss once told me. "You don't want to just pop the question out of the blue. You've got to start dropping a few hints. Test the waters. Make sure they're going to say yes. Make sure they're going to say, 'I thought you'd never ask!'" But like all marriage proposals, there's always the risk of miscalculation, the risk of drama. And in the world of recruiting spies, drama is best handled in private.

I run a surveillance detection route from the airport to be sure I don't have a tail. Taxi to a dress shop, **tuk-tuk** to the island's new mall, exit on foot to jump a **songthaew** the rest of the way. It's brief yet effective. I could throw in a few more stops, but it's obvious

I'm not covered and I'd rather get to the room early to be sure the layout is right. Better to find suites where the sitting room has a door to block any view of the bed. Helps avoid sending mixed signals. This one is perfect.

I unzip my backpack and pull out a few art books I've brought in case we get interrupted and need to explain the purpose of our meeting. Then I fill up my little Zen fountain with water from the bathroom sink and plug it in. It's a strange piece of gear to carry but more elegant than turning on the bathroom taps. Running water makes the best sound-masking since it can't be replicated, the way television programs or music can. On the off chance that this room is wired for audio surveillance, the Thai service could look up any TV show that was playing and cancel it out to improve the quality of the recording. But water flows differently every time—there's no way to replicate it and reclaim the lost conversation beneath. That, and it makes for a much more calming accompaniment to a recruitment pitch than the blinking buzzers and bells of late-night Asian TV.

I check my watch. Jakab will be here soon. If he were an established asset, I'd be arranging the blinds in such a way as to signal to him, on the street, that it's safe to come up.

But he hasn't been recruited yet. We have no secret commo plan, no agreed-upon language of signals to exchange. For now, it's still old-fashioned phone calls. I tell him the suite number and put the Do Not Disturb sign on the door.

When he arrives, he is singing. I can hear him coming down the hall. It's a shame he'll have to stop doing that. I rather like the lilt of his voice. But it's not the most secure way to approach a clandestine meeting, crooning to the heavens for everyone to hear.

When I open the door, I'm startled, as I always am, at how little his face resembles his voice. He greets me in accented English. His diction has a stickiness to it, like he's just eaten a spoonful of peanut butter. He kisses the air beside my left cheek, then my right. He smells of aftershave and sweat.

"Any problem finding the place?" I ask as I grab him a beer. It's the first in a sequence of questions I'll ask more formally at the start of every meeting once he's fully recruited. They go by an acronym: STINC, which stands for Security (Any run-ins with the local service on your way here?), Time (How long do we have?), Intelligence (Any emergency information to share?), Next meeting (If we get interrupted, when can we meet back up?), and Cover (Here's the reason we're together right now, should anyone happen to ask). I can't be quite so overt with Jakab just yet, so I knead the questions a bit until they feel more conversational and doughy. He sits and answers with hand gestures and grunts, his legs outstretched and crossed at the ankle, his beer balanced on the arm of his chair.

"I brought some materials about our newest crop of artists," I finish, reviewing our ostensible reason for meeting. He nods without looking at the books. "This one uses casts of artifacts from Hiroshima." I point to an image on one of the pages. "Wristwatches frozen in time. Shreds of school uniforms burned off the backs of schoolchildren as they ran."

"Can I smoke?" he asks.

"Of course." I open the window to keep the fire alarm from squawking but leave the gauzy drape pulled shut. "Stressful month?" By now I've realized that Jakab is that endearing brand of hard-ass who is perpetually quitting cigarettes but never seems to succeed. I have an ashtray on the launchpad.

"Fuck. The Hungarian economy. No jobs, nothing. And still the government spends." He whistles, like he's watching a pile of cash on fire. "So much spending you can't believe it."

"Must be frustrating," I say. He looks up at me as he lights his cigarette.

"Goddamn sponge pigs," he says, exhaling the first drag. "Racking up debt same as the Communists. No better. They're all crooks."

"They should be looking out for you. That's their job, the government. To take care of the people." I know he will laugh, and he does.

"Nobody's taking care of us but us," he says.

"Your people should be so lucky."

"Huh?" he asks.

"To have you taking care of them."

"Oh," he laughs. "Sure. Well, not much I can do beyond taking care of myself."

I let it hang there for a minute. This perfect opening. This big, fat "if only" hanging in the room like a Nintendo power-up, just suspended there for the taking.

"What if there were?"

He holds my eye contact while he inhales, then exhales. He's waiting for me to elaborate. For a beat or two, I let him. He's mush on the inside, really. Gentle and protective. More like his voice than his face.

"Those special channels I mentioned having to Washington," I say. "The friends I talk to there. What if we could work together to take care of your people? To take care of you."

He stares at me a beat longer. Then he laughs.

"You have confused me with Batman," he says.

I crack a grin. "No confusion, Jakab. You hold life and death in your hands, no? You're not selling encyclopedias."

"Military surplus."

"Nuclear precursors," I correct him gently.

"Half of it doesn't even work." He lights another cigarette. "What does that help my people anyway?"

"You think they're never going to use one of those things in Europe? You put this stuff out there in the world, you sell to people who kill civilians, kill young people, who's to say their next target won't be in your hometown?"

He rolls his eyes. "Hungary doesn't participate in this worthless war. No one has any reason to hurt us," he says.

I edge my seat closer to his and lock into his gaze. "If they use one of these things anywhere, it's going to hurt you, Jakab. What do you think's going to happen to that horrible economy you were talking about if a terrorist group detonates a dirty bomb or a tactical nuke? Even if it's halfway around the globe. It's going to make today's economy look like the boom times. And all the people you know back home—the ones who are just holding on—they're going to get taken to the woodshed. People will be jobless. People will be homeless. People will be desperate. And desperate people make violent choices. What goes around comes around, Jakab. You get to decide. You get to write your country's future. Sell your people out or save them like the heroes of those songs you always sing. It's your call."

He's not smoking now. He's just staring at the lit end of his cigarette, head-on, like there are answers rolled in there.

"You want me to stop selling." He mulls it over. "Who d'you work for? CIA?"

"Not stop, exactly. And yes, I work for CIA."

He looks up at me. I resist the temptation to fill the silence.

"So, what? I have to work with you or you arrest me?"

"Nothing like that, Jakab. I respect you far too much to pull anything like that. Look. We're friends. I know you. I know that your grandfather was killed when Communists took over your country. I know that you don't trust big government. I know what you want for your people. The freedom to live a good life. To work a good job and be left alone. I get it. I want that, too. And that's not what happens when the whole world is at war.

That's not what happens when people are afraid. What happens is more government, not less. More laws, more prisons, more executions. We're in a unique position, you and I. We're two friends who happen to have contacts in special places. You know the groups trying to buy this stuff, and I know the people trying to stop them. Together, we can make sure you never worry about the economy again. We can make sure your family never wants for food or medicine or education again. But more than that, we can work to make the world a little less like the one that killed your grandfather and a little more like the one you want your boys to inherit."

"A pretty speech," he says in his sticky voice, but I can hear that he wants to believe it.

"Jakab, if not us, who? If not now, when? Archimedes said, 'Give me a lever and a place to stand and I will move the world.' Well, you and I, we have that lever and that place to stand. We can save thousands, maybe millions of lives. We can make people a little less afraid. Because it's only fearful people who tolerate the kind of government you hate. Fear empowers fascism, and together we can make the world a little less fearful, Jakab. That doesn't happen every day."

There is a beat of silence. And then he looks

up at me with the eyes of a believer. "What exactly are you asking me to do?"

We're over the hump now.

"We'll work that out together. It's going to depend on the moment. You'll tell me about your business, who your buyers are, what they're interested in buying and why. Then together we'll decide the best way to make sure your weapons don't go boom."

"They'll kill me," he says. This great goliath of a man, struggling with the prospect of sharing his grandfather's fate.

"I won't let that happen, Jakab. Think about it. I've been protecting you for almost a year now. Making sure we haven't been seen together in public. Staying off text messages. Keeping our phone calls vague. You may not have realized it, but I've had your back for a long time now, preparing everything in case you wanted to jump to the light side. You're my friend first, Jakab. You have a family. I have a family. We're in this together. Because otherwise it could be our kids who have the uniforms burned off their backs." I can feel the movement beneath my navel, a flutter of forming arms and legs to remind me that I'm not kidding.

"How does it work?" he asks. "How often would I see you?"

"As often as you get a weapons order. Or

Life Undercover

a shipment. As often as you want to tell me something."

"How do I contact you?"

I pull out a Starbucks gift card. "If you need me, buy a latte. Then meet me here twenty-four hours later. If it's an emergency, call me. When I pick up, ask to speak to Marina. I'll tell you you've got the wrong number. You hang up. And I'll call you back from a secure line."

"Do I get paid?"

"You get to tell your grandkids you saved the world for them." He looks at me like he can't eat bragging rights. "And I'll make sure you get compensated for your time. One thousand dollars a month to start. Let's see how it goes."

He sits still for a minute. No cigarette, no beer, no words. And in that silence, I know he's working his way toward yes.

"Don't get me killed," he says.

"Deal," I say. And I take out a piece of paper with the terms of our agreement typed in Courier font. It specifies that Jakab will be working with the CIA. It outlines the fee he will be paid and the expenses for which he will be reimbursed. At the bottom there is a blank line for each of us to sign. It's a strange piece of fiction, the idea that I would ever

walk onto the street with this most incriminating of documents, signed and executed
between me and an arms dealer. But the
signing of names carries psychological heft,
and so headquarters likes us to go through
the motions to cement the commitment,
even though I'll destroy the paper as soon as
he leaves. I lay the document on the table and
raise my beer in the air. I haven't drunk any,
but Jakab doesn't know I'm pregnant and
assets don't like to drink alone, so I keep up
the masquerade.

"To your grandfather," I say. "May he be
watching."

"And to our grandchildren," he says. "May
they survive."

He hugs me. A sudden bear hug followed
by a return to formality. Then he signs up to
stop a nuclear winter with the blue ink of a
cheap hotel pen.

After he leaves, I fold the document into
pleats, like the geisha fans we used to make in
elementary school. Then I set the accordion
on its end atop the toilet bowl water and light
it on fire. It's an old Russia House trick to
keep the smoke to a minimum and contain
the ash. When our agreement is converted
to floating black flakes, I flush and set about
packing up the books and the beer and the

fountain. I walk out the back of the hotel, onto the beach. The place Dean and I are staying is on this same strip of sand. The moon is bright and the music is pulsing and I pull off my shoes to walk in the surf on my way to find him. For a few minutes, it all seems possible. Preventing nuclear war. Making my marriage real. Going all in.

Then I get to our empty hotel room to find a hastily scrawled note: "Had to go work. See you at home."

17

Back in Shanghai, the silence sets in once more. Dean and I have been together for a couple of years at this point, but we've spent most of those years separated by oceans and deserts and mountains, working different operations in different war zones. Though we technically shared our little home in Virginia, we were both traveling too much to know the familiarity that grows from the prolonged sharing of space. Shanghai is the first time we've truly lived in the same house in the same city, and every habit, every tic, every turn of phrase is unfamiliar. Each day, we playact at marital bliss for the watching eyes. Each day, we feel more heavily the truth that we are strangers. I curl up in the evenings on the old daybed in the corner of our lane house and watch him play pirated video games, searching his face for some way in, some way to know him. And each day, like a cosmic ticking clock, the life we've made together grows beneath my navel, asking me, from the inside out, to make our family real before he or she is born.

I'm not sure if Dean regrets leaving Afghanistan or regrets going there to begin with. Don't know whether the frustration that simmers beneath the edge in his voice is trauma or longing. I question whether the fact that he's killed means he needs to believe in war. Wonder if he remembers I became a spy to wage peace.

I can't ask him any of this aloud, because the walls are listening. So I shift to the world of double meaning. A touch on the wrist here, a coded reference there. And in response, his voice changes, a hardness creeps in. It's like attempting communication inside a Dalí painting, with every detail interpretable a dozen ways and no master glossary to keep us from traveling universes apart.

On my return from Thailand, my stomach beginning to swell with four months of new life, we cook spaghetti Bolognese. Dean knows that the babymoon was a cover but has no idea what the operation really might have been or whether it succeeded.

"How was the collection?" he asks.

"Important," I reply, touching his hand as

he gives the sauté pan a jerk. "Really interesting investigation of peace."

"Those exhibitions all strike me as phony," he says, pouring the meat sauce over the noodles as Ayi tidies the kitchen beside us.

"This one felt different," I say.

"Don't they always?" He walks out of the kitchen, carrying our plates.

I follow him. Ayi follows me.

"The artist's point is that we should never stop trying," I say as I take a bite.

"Sounds like the artist is a child," he says. We chew in silence.

"Or a mother," I answer. The maid brings over a plate of candies.

"Sucker?" he says, offering me a lollipop.

I excuse myself, walk into the bathroom, and close the door. Three months later, a debriefer at Langley asks me what made me cry that night; the question is supported by a surveillance photo, taken from the vicinity of the bathroom mirror, that shows my eyes closed, silent tears carving their slow way down my cheeks, my hands at rest on the curve of my unborn child.

"Morning sickness," I tell him. "You guys are watching us over there?"

"Nope, they are," he says. "We're just watching them."

Dean buys pirated video games set in the same region he was deployed to back in Afghanistan. I know he misses it. I know how good he was at it. I know he gave it up to be with me. I want to tell him I'm sorry he's stuck in this remote prison of silence, far away from his colleagues and watering holes and adrenaline-soaked purpose. But I can't say any of that out loud. So instead, we live in something like spiritual silence, watching **Project Runway** and **Entourage,** a pantomime of normality between surveillance routes and dead drops and covert cables to HQS in anachronistic all caps.

There is a wall between us, and we can't follow the age-old advice—communicate!—because we're explicitly forbidden from saying anything that might suggest vulnerability in our marriage anywhere in-country. We take walks sometimes, when the tension becomes unbearable, around lakes in parks, my hands on my rounded belly as we talk out of the sides of our mouths. And every few months we return to D.C., and the countless points of friction come tumbling out of us, like air rushing from a balloon, only to dissipate unprocessed amid the joy of being home and the swirl of HQS debriefings.

The surge in Iraq has worked to turn the

tide against al Qa'ida for the time being, and most of my operations are in other countries now, tracking brokers via Jakab and the others in his network. It never stops haunting my dreams, the potential for Hiroshima on our watch. Many of the deals we track are scams. Organized crime syndicates get rich selling harmless "red mercury" the way high school drug dealers make their pocket money peddling oregano. Even the technology that's real is usually incomplete or broken by the time it passes hands. Or too complex to operate without a team of experts and a government cleanroom. But all it takes is one—one little nuke in a suitcase and 9/11 would look like the opening act.

Six months into the pregnancy, I begin feeling the baby's hiccups around the same time every day, like little internal question marks. Should a future mom really be out preventing the sale of WMDs to terrorists? Could a future mom possibly choose not to?

In between operations, I curl up in Dean's arms back in the silence of Shanghai. We still don't really know each other, but we both know the life growing inside me. This child is the only truth we share completely. Dean holds my hand during each prenatal visit. One day, he doesn't even drop it when we get to the privacy of the taxi. "How about that heartbeat?" he asks.

We're so used to expressing fake emotions over fake dinner conversations about days spent at fake art fairs that the realness of it startles me.

"Beautiful," I say.

"Strong." He nods.

"Wonder when it beat for the first time," I muse, watching the Shanghai streets blur by, ducks and chickens strung across alleyways and families balancing on motor scooters. "Crazy it was just a bunch of matter hanging out in my body, and then it got made into a heart. And then that heart started beating. It's pretty incredible, right? That we made life?"

Soon, we learn that our baby is a girl. "Wonder woman," Dean says. I'm relieved, especially given how hard it was to find out, securing a special dispensation to ask our child's gender. In a country where many parents are still permitted only one child, boys are prized for their future earning potential, and the Chinese government is trying to prevent families from aborting their female babies by keeping fetal gender a state-mandated secret until birth. It's a security issue for them. Twentysomething men now outnumber women so dramatically, Beijing has opened a new class of visas for single Southeast Asian women. Married men are less likely to protest in Tiananmen Square, or so the logic goes.

We start to incorporate baby shops into our surveillance detection routes, oohing and aahing over soft pink blankets and stuffed furry animals while watching the door for Chinese intelligence officers trailing us to see if we're operational. Dean's home more often now. He's cut down on his ops schedule to be sure he'll be around when the baby comes. The waiting makes him antsy. He fills the lane house with a kind of energetic turbulence, thrashing against the stillness with CrossFit workouts and video games. But between the simulated battles of the Xbox and the actual violence of his sleep, he finds peace in the blurry crystal ball of the ultrasound pictures.

"Do you think she has my nose?" he asks, holding the flimsy printout up to the light. I run facial recognition software between Dean's photo and the grainy scan.

"Twenty-four percent match!" I announce, laughing.

"Hey, that's enough, right?" It's a reference to how low the threshold is for the United States to render a suspect to a black site or Guantánamo. This is the first time I've heard

Dean acknowledge the injustice of some renditions. I crawl across the daybed.

"I love you," I tell him, not for show.

The last time we're in Washington before my due date, I suggest that we update our E&E plan. Every CIA operative has one—an "escape and evasion plan" covering how to get out of the country if everything goes to hell. The current plan we have on file involves an extremely long swim, along with some overnights under piles of leaves and a few other stretches that don't seem especially practical with an infant in tow. "We'll have to think about that," comes the reply. "Never had anyone deliver a baby while under nonofficial cover."

When I see my mother, she suggests: "Maybe you should have her in the States."

"Mom, millions of babies are born in China," I counter. "That's where my art business is."

Not for the first time and not for the last, my mother's words would soon ring in my ears.

—

I go into labor in Shanghai on the first of September 2008—Labor Day, as it turns out, fresh after the end of the Chinese Olympics, with homemade fireworks still bursting outside the hospital windows, bright reds and oranges against the billowing blackness of smoke. My mom and sisters are there. The previous day, my mother came over and rode a bicycle in circles around our living room floor while Dean cooked dinner. I had never loved her more. This impossibly beautiful human, whose body pulled me together from nothing and whose spirit electrified me with everything. I went to bed, as early contractions took hold, conscious of one single prayer: "Lord, let me be my mother."

A few hours into labor, the nurses suggest Pitocin and the baby's heartbeat begins to race. Immediately the medical team switches from Mandarin, which I somewhat understand, to Shanghainese, which I don't. I resist the temptation to ask them to translate, knowing it will slow them down, and the medical training I have is only field triage—tying of tourniquets and removal of shrapnel. They rush me to an operating theater, give me an epidural, and pull our daughter, purple and milky, from an incision in my stomach. Dean captures it, **National Geographic** photographer that he is. And the hardest twelve hours of my life begin. Gazing at my crumpled daughter tucked into an acrylic container beside my bed, I'm still paralyzed from the neck down—I can't hold her, can't move a single finger, though I try with the might I imagine it would take to lift a car. They tell me it's a side effect of a hastily executed emergency epidural. They say I should regain feeling in the next forty-eight hours. I've never heard of that happening. Flooded with drugs and hormones, I don't believe them.

In my woozy mind's eye, I see images of Alexander Litvinenko, dying in his hospital bed after Russian intelligence dosed him with radioactive poison. I run through possibilities, a covert operative lying helpless in a hostile country. Has Beijing gotten to the nurses? Or Moscow? Or Tehran? Is it safe to sleep? Will I wake? Will I hold my daughter? Or is this it for me now? Am I a paraplegic, forever frozen out of the real life I barely got to taste?

I fall asleep and wake up in the same room in my dream. "I can't hold her," I say, "my arms don't work." "Don't worry," I hear my own voice reply, "we have so many arms. Look, there's another pair of our arms there." In the dream, I'm watching a nurse arrive and scoop my daughter into her arms. And suddenly I am my daughter, looking up into this nurse's eyes. And I am also the nurse, looking down

at this face, not one hour old. And I'm looking at myself, nurse to baby, baby to nurse,
and thinking how smart the person is who
invented the mirror or how else would life
see itself, and I remember the thing Kallistos
Ware said, the Greek Orthodox priest from
my college at Oxford, with the robes and the
beard and the big, heavy cross—"In the end,
Amaryllis, it's as Saint Augustine said: the
entire universe is just Christ, loving himself."
And then it goes dark.

The next day, before I even open my eyes,
I try to move my fingers. They brush against
my palm, creaky but obedient. I am flooded
with relief and, for the first time, scoop my
daughter into my arms.

—

We name her Zoë Victoria, meaning "Life
triumphs." It's the simplest devotion I can
think of, testimony to the resilience of life,
of love, of light against death and fear and
darkness.

My mother and sisters leave and Dean, Zoë,
and I return to the Shanghai lane house. We
playact at being a normal family for the cameras and the microphones and quiet old Ayi,

who reports back to Beijing. Only nobody has briefed Zoë on the mission, and she doesn't play her role right, doesn't do the things in the books on the day that she's meant to. And deep inside my stoic, silent exterior, I begin to panic, begin to crawl in my skin the way my mom had with Ben before his particular brand of genius emerged. Eye contact, the book says, that's the first experience you'll share. But we don't. Not at all. And the harder I try, the more diligently my daughter avoids locking windows and granting me access to her soul.

It's a new feeling, this Hydra in my gut. Counterterrorism, no problem. Counterproliferation, piece of cake. But this tiny infant creature's distant gaze leaves me pale and panicked. I jump to conclusions. I stop eating. I pore over Internet forums and self-diagnose, make bargains with God, until finally, uninvited, Dean takes my hand. He says, quite simply, "Babies are unpredictable—let's let her lead." It is simple and strong, like a stone obelisk I can see through the fog, and I let the fear go a little and hold on to Zoë instead.

Slowly I ramp back up to my normal pace of operations, flying overseas with Zoë wrapped against my body, while I work to prevent imminent attacks. Never to war zones, but meeting arms dealers turned sources in any country carries risks and I work with a new, almost obsessive care. I run foreign surveillance detection routes with her strapped to my chest. Take notes after secret car meetings with her snoring gently under my chin, tuck papers into concealment devices stuffed with her diapers to relay back to HQS via my covert communications device in the darkness of home. Each time, I weigh the danger of wherever I'm going against the danger of leaving my infant daughter without me in a hostile country, where the housekeeper works for the security service. There's the ever-present temptation to choose neither, to throw in the towel and head for the safety of retirement and home, but with each new threat, there are the conjured faces of those children—just as innocent as mine—whose lives hang in the balance. Babies in their strollers in the parks of New York City and London, Bangkok and Istanbul.

Between operations, I sit with her at the Buddhist temple in Shanghai, watching the old women feed the koi fish offerings. Here is a fragment of me, living outside my body. A fragment of me I can't compel to pretend to be normal, pretend to be anything. A fragment of me independent and new enough to refuse to play some game of make-believe.

"I get it," I tell her. "You're not the theoretical baby in the book, who makes eye contact on day one. You're Zoë, who makes eye contact when she believes there's something real to see. You're a raw human spirit in a tiny, brand-new spaceship, searching for the soul that is your mom. And so far, your sensors haven't found her. I don't blame you, you know. I'm not sure where she is, either."

I make sure nobody can hear us, and then I talk to her about being afraid. I talk to her about wanting to be known. I talk to her about the night in the hotel bathroom and my dream the night she was born. I tell her all kinds of things I've never said aloud, or even inside my own head. And she looks out at the middle distance mostly, when she's not snoring or guzzling my milk.

Then one day, sitting at the temple, I lose my train of thought, completely absorbed in following a koi as he nibbles the pellet offerings bobbing on the water. I'm smiling, without meaning to, and instead of returning to my confessions, I say, absentmindedly, "We probably look really weird to that fish, huh, Zoë?" And when I look down, her eyes find mine and she smiles.

For a moment, I forget to worry about who I am and who I am pretending to be. And I see through the eyes of a fish. By accident, really. And in that moment, my daughter's sensors find me, her real mom, fear and anxiety stripped away, childlike and joyful, seeing the fish-eye view of things, just as easily as can be.

I start laughing. And she starts laughing. Her huge green-brown eyes looking steadily back into mine. And I'm flooded by a sudden, forceful wellspring of connection, like I'm experiencing eternity. And the old woman who sweeps the grounds starts laughing too, with stained, ancient teeth. "Welcome out of head," she says. I look at her quizzically. "Beautiful day," she adds and grins, gesturing to the sky.

And so it is that I learn that Zoë sees me when I forget myself, that I'm real only when I'm not aware of being anything at all, which simultaneously makes sense and no sense whatsoever. Guess that's what I get for hanging out beneath a giant smiling Buddha. "Joke's on us," I say to Zoë, as we get up to walk home.

—

I've never underestimated the danger of living undercover in a hostile country. I've spent the days of my career in a hyperfocused present, knowing in my quiet subconscious, when I hear about this upcoming election or that movie due out in the spring, that I might not be around to see how it turns out. There's no drama in this. It's simply been my reality, in the way we all understand that we might not live to see humans walk on Mars. My time frame has just been a little shorter. The reality of the work.

But my daughter's hand closes tightly around my finger when I hold her now, and life seems harder to part with than it used to. As I walk the Shanghai streets, I watch the street sellers who spy on us with a swelling dread, equal and opposite to the swelling love with which I watch her. I feel the magnitude of what could be taken from us and how painful it would be to endure.

As the weather warms, I start working outside in our walled garden, where I'm less aware of the cameras and Zoë can watch the birds beside me. Still, Ayi hovers about us like a mist, so we are never quite free of Beijing.

One morning, I eat breakfast while making some notes at the garden table. Ayi sweeps the ground close enough to sneak glances at my scrawl. The notes are fabricated, intended to reinforce my cover as an art dealer. I scribble fictions, and she hovers behind me to consume them. Zoë bats at a mobile, suspended over her bouncy chair.

"Preparing for the India Art Fair," I say. Ayi nods, stony-faced. Zoë turns away.

We've done this dance a hundred times. I lie. Ayi lets me. But something about Zoë's response makes me set down my pen. I turn my face up to Ayi's. She's blank and hard.

Without knowing I'm going to say it until I hear my own words in the air, I ask her, "Do you ever get scared?"

She startles, as if she's walked through a cobweb. Then she nods.

"Yeah, me too," I say. Zoë turns toward us and gives the mobile a pat. "I'm scared I won't be a good mom."

Ayi sits down. She hasn't done that before.

"I'm scared I'm not beautiful to my husband anymore," she says.

We talk for a minute longer, enthralled by each other's realness. Then a gap in the conversation lasts a beat too long for comfort and we fall back into our respective suits of armor. She stands up, hard again. But as she picks up the broom, she says, "If you need privacy, the second-floor bathroom is quiet."

We've suspected for a while that the second-floor bathroom isn't wired for surveillance. That doesn't surprise me. It's the gruff confirmation that knocks the breath out of me, volunteered from haunting, hostile Ayi. She nods one more time, as if to confirm her capacity for independent decisions, and shuffles inside. I turn to Zoë, with eyes that say, "Well, would ya look at that!" It's probably my imagination, but Zoë's delighted smile seems to say, "I told you so."

Like a tiny, wrinkled Yoda, Zoë teaches me to use that Force, turning her little eyes away when I start projecting my cover story, lighting up when I drop the act. Like any clumsy Jedi apprentice, I struggle to control it at first. Can't access the raw humanness on demand, can't steer it when I do. Half the time, I'm not sure I want to. I'm undercover in a hard-target country, after all. Not the best time for radical honesty. But oddly, the more I practice, the more I find that letting my guard down and climbing inside the realness of other people makes me feel more secure, not less.

It happens next during a tense meal with Dean at a restaurant in Shanghai. I've heard via my covcom that Jakab has information about a planned attack in Karachi. His buyers in the al Qa'ida affiliates there may want to try their hand at a dirty bomb—an explosive device laced with fissile uranium to coat everything it doesn't destroy with radiation. Dirty bombs are more a tool of mass disruption than mass destruction. They don't trigger an actual nuclear reaction, so they're unlikely to add more than a few hundred to the casualty count. But they still make the vicinity of the attack uninhabitable for years, possibly decades. And any use of uranium would cause a worldwide panic. For a terror group perpetually in search of headlines, that makes it a gateway drug. Next stop: a suitcase nuke or a full-on ten-kiloton weapon in the streets of New York. We know they've already been inquiring. It's the path we work day and night to stop al Qa'ida from treading. And from Jakab's note, it sounds like they're about to take the first step.

The problem is, I can't take the baby to Pakistan. It's been classified as a war zone for the purposes of family-deployment guidelines. But the timeline is too short and the potential cost too high to try stopping the attack long-distance. I've got to be on the ground. It will be my first time away from Zoë since she was born.

Dean and I sit in a restaurant in Shanghai and discuss it in clumsy layers of code, a parallel universe where artists are terrorists and paintings are weapons.

"It's a tough market there," he says, and I nod. "You're never going to convince these guys to stop collecting. Just switch out the Munch with a Matisse and hope they don't notice." He means Edvard Munch, the painter of **The Scream,** that hellish, flat depiction of a nightmare sunset, etched around the hollow face of our most ghoulish selves. Human annihilation, drawn in oil on cardboard. I know he means a nuclear weapon. And the bucolic calm of Matisse is a nuclear attack avoided. He's suggesting that we switch out the uranium with an inert blob of clay.

"They'll notice when they hang it," I say.

"So fuck 'em," he answers, ripping a piece of bread in two.

"Our guy isn't the only art broker in the world. If they think he screwed them, they'll just go find a Munch somewhere else." And kill Jakab in the process, I add with my eyes. Dean looks like that wouldn't be the worst thing.

"Brokers who sell stolen paintings aren't your friends," he says, and I grimace. It's not the best idea to talk about theft, even in the coded context of art. Beijing is just as liable to arrest foreigners for business fraud as they are for espionage. I glance around us, but all seems quiet.

"Maybe not, but he's our partner. We need to protect him." We fall silent as the waiter brings our crepes. He is French and bulbous-nosed, as though he has enjoyed a few too many bottles of Bordeaux in his time. He arranges our plates in front of us with a flourish, then returns to the kitchen.

"I can use a different artist to introduce me to the buyers," I continue. "He'll tell them I'm from the museum. Just play it straight and leave Jakab out of it." The museum is what we call the U.S. government. The other artist I have in mind is a terror cell go-between we've worked with in the past—a courier the al Qa'ida affiliates trust to broker conversations on Pakistani soil.

"You're gonna walk right in there and say you're from the museum," he says, and I nod. "Why wouldn't I go, then?" he asks. "If cover doesn't matter."

"You're too threatening," I reply. I intend it as a compliment. And besides, it's true.

"You mean I'm a thug," he says.

"No, I mean you have a track record over there."

"Damn right I do."

He tucks his shoulders up and inward,

like he's bracing for a fight, like he feels challenged, vulnerable, endangered. The waiter interrupts us to refill our water, and as we pause again, I find myself plunged hard into Dean's perspective, as if I've been dunked beneath rough ocean waves and the secret life beneath the surface is coming dimly into focus. I feel the hollowness that was created when he gave up his career path for mine, leaving the battlefield he had mastered so we could deploy here together, with none of the immediacy a war zone could offer, no opportunity to take down the adversary with night-vision goggles and a tricked-out M4. This more subtle, secret form of combat—this Tao of recruiting your enemy—leaves him less certain that he's made his country safer, less certain that he's done his job at all. I feel how exhausting it is to know that his wife and daughter are at risk when he's awake and to relive explosions and beheadings when he sleeps. I swell with admiration for him—for his skill on the battlefield and his honor at home. I reach across the table and take his hand.

That night, we make love. And the boundaries of our safe, pragmatic distance begin to melt.

18

Before I leave for Karachi, I hold Zoë for a long time, standing in the hallway, pouring wordless messages into her. Then I roll her into Dean's arms without waking her, press my forehead to his for a moment, and walk into the alleyway, under the drying fish and out onto the street. My vision's blurry with questions and maybe also with tears. How can I walk away from my daughter, knowing that I might not return? How could I stay, knowing that I can stop an attack that will kill another version of her, half a world away, a little girl in the United States or Pakistan whose mother sent her off to school with the same wordless love? A few days away from Zoë to prevent a wound to the world she will inherit. It's parenting the best way I know how. But it's all I can do to get myself up the train station stairs.

As the city sprawls itself outside the train window, I pack the aching part of me away and steel myself for work. It hasn't occurred to me yet that love can be a superpower in the field. It still feels like a giant chink in my armor, the smell of my daughter that lingers where I just held her against my shoulder. Vulnerability is well and good at home, but I'm headed to the airport now, bound for a room full of men with whom my country is at war. Men whose organization has killed friends I love. I tuck my fear and weakness and thoughts of Zoë beneath a veneer of tough indifference, slip back into my protective armor and lock layer upon layer of defensive deceptions down tight.

When I land in Pakistan, I climb into a taxi and fire up the covert communications system concealed within my phone to check in with headquarters. There's a cable waiting, filled with bureaucratic red tape. HOLD ALL FIELD OPS UNTIL FURTHER NOTICE, it concludes. I bristle at the delay it's going to cause. I'm here to prevent a major and imminent attack. One that could kill children. One that's taken me away from my own child. It's no time to get put on ice. **Shows what these guys know about the field**, I think, cranking up the old diatribe in my head—the one so familiar to all field operatives when faced with administrative hurdles from Langley. **I don't even know the guy who wrote this cable,** I think. **He's probably a trainee. Probably enjoying a nice Dunkin' Donuts cruller from the HQS cafeteria. Typical CYA.** "CYA" stands for "cover your ass," the barb we throw at anyone who tries to slow us down with pesky permissions and paperwork. I'm alone and operational in the country where Danny was taken and beheaded, and every hour I'm delayed is another hour for something to go wrong—for an informant to disclose my location, for the source I'm meeting to cancel, for the attack to go boom. The fear injects my thoughts with venom. **Beltway BS. No wonder we're losing this war. Bunch of risk-averse desk jockeys calling the shots.** The taxi jerks to a stop at an intersection, and I look up. The plastic back of the driver's seat is covered in graffiti. Most of it is in Urdu. Some is in Arabic. One creased sticker off to the side is in English. It says, "Remember the other person is you."

I stare at it. And then I laugh. "Hi, Zoë," I say out loud.

"What is it, lady?" the driver asks.

"Nothing," I tell him, and look back at my phone. I reread the cable and begrudgingly notice this time the care the author took to acknowledge the importance of the operation and to express his regret at the delay his request will cause. I remember sitting at the desk in my Virginia safe house, running point for these same kinds of operations before I deployed. Remember the gnawing fear that an officer would be lost on my watch, the responsibility I felt to protect them, even if that meant slowing them down. I imagine the desk guy again, still with a doughnut, but also with good intentions. I imagine his family members at home, resenting his absence, the way Anthony resented mine. I feel what it's costing that officer to make sure I'm safe.

COPY, WILL COMPLY, I tap reluctantly into the response cable. APPRECIATE YOU HAVING MY BACK.

The delay, I understand as I pay the cabbie and head into the temporary apartment that's been arranged for me, means twenty-four fewer hours for casing and prep. Instead of checking out the lay of the land, I'm confined to the indoors until I get the all clear.

I spend the rest of the day on the cinderblock balcony, watching the flow of the street beneath. The women wear Islamic dress, gesticulating and laughing as they gossip their way through the vegetable stalls. The boys play cricket, darting into traffic in pursuit of the ball. Young people put sugar in their tea and gather to chat outside the community center after evening services. In the midst of the dust and heat and noise, there are the recognizable patterns of everyday existence. The unremarkable passing of a day that makes life everywhere so beautiful.

Just after the final call to prayer, I receive word back from headquarters: ADDITIONAL CHECKS ARE NOW COMPLETE. YOU ARE CLEARED TO PROCEED. GODSPEED. It isn't until later that night that I see the news. A CIA operative has been killed by a suicide bomber across the border in Afghanistan. I understand now why they wanted to execute additional checks before I walk into the meeting tomorrow. I would have asked them to do the same, had I known what they knew. I jerk in and out of fitful sleep, hurting for the dead and for the kids who'll grow up without them. The Dunkin' Donuts desk officers, I figure, must be blaming themselves. I'm relieved that I gave them the benefit of the doubt.

The Pakistani dawn creeps through the blinds in slices of orange, accompanied by clangs and honks and whiffs of slow-cooking meat. The plan for today is to case the intersection Jakab's given me for the intended attack, then go to the meeting tomorrow, armed with a better understanding of the target. I flatten a tourist map from the airport across the bed and trace a stairstep path through the city with my finger. The more turns in a surveillance detection route, the better. Each time I change directions, I get one precious chance to glance behind myself, one glimpse as I cross the road to pick out any potential surveillant, any person I've seen repeatedly as I wind my way across town.

On the off chance that I'm being watched, the route has to look natural—an M-shaped shopping trip across the city with unusual destinations at each turning point to offer a plausible explanation for taking each leg. Those anchor points usually require some casing, but having lost twenty-four hours to the bureaucratic hold, I only have time to ballpark it based on the map. Its little cartoon buildings mark points Karachi tour guides think might be of interest. I pick out a few that are likely to be open, with the requisite mess of back-alley turns to stairstep my way in between. Clifton Beach, the zoo, back down to Jodia Bazar and over to the intersection of Abdullah Haroon and Sarwar Shaheed—the corner where the attack is planned to take place.

—

My route starts out smoothly enough. The upscale boutiques and Chinese restaurants of Clifton spit me out by the water. The beach is broad here and scalloped by great, wide arcs where the Arabian Sea has washed the sand with silver. Families walk in the waves, their kameezes salt-stained and waterlogged around their calves, the children delighted despite the heavy wetness of their clothes. Teenagers on motorcycles cruise along the beach, their 70cc engines struggling against the sand. I choose a restaurant with entrances on both the street and the water sides, forcing any surveillant I might have to follow me inside. None does. I order a fruit juice and sit for a moment, watching the ocean come and go. The kids are flying kites.

No sign of surveillance so far. No one is watching me as I watch the water. No one follows me as I climb into a taxi and head to the zoo. When I get there, I stop in front of a concrete enclosure the size of a small train car. Inside, alone on the cement floor, is a lion. His mane hangs sparse and dingy from his face, like a threadbare and forgotten stuffed toy. I wonder if he's given up or if there's fight left in him, a memory of freedom.

Out of the corner of my eye, I see what might be someone using a cell phone to take a photo. Normally that would send up a red flag, but zoos are tourist territory. Probably just someone clocking animals for their scrapbook. Poor old lion. Only thing worse than enduring a life of loneliness and concrete is being photographed by those who run free.

I wander through the remaining exhibits—elephants and zebras, even a herd of gazelle-type things I suppose must still tread savannahs in their dreams. It's a soul-crushing place, this park of concrete cages. Back out in the cacophony of Nishtar Road, I jump into a motorized rickshaw. The afternoon is hot and the fumes are foul, but I can't stand the confined enclosure of a taxi or a bus just now.

The driver seems to harbor the same need for speed. He slams a hard right and careens off the main drag into a labyrinth of back roads. We skirt food stalls and water buffalo, whip around construction equipment and games of street ball. Motorbikes screech in front of us, and glass bottles crunch under our wheels. It's like Mr. Toad's Wild Ride, only with no seat belts and a fairly significant chance of death.

It used to be standard operating procedure not to wear seat belts in hostile environments, just in case an officer needed to bail during an ambush. Then the statisticians pointed out that we were losing more operatives to car accidents than terrorist attacks, and we went back to "Click It or Ticket."

I think of Zoë and signal to the driver that I'll jump out at the next corner. We're at the edge of Jodia Market. I can walk the rest of the way.

The stalls around me are staffed by grain sellers, mainly, and spice traders, their sacks of curry and cumin rolled open to fill the air with scent.

Halfway to the vegetables, I notice someone behind me. Once, then again around the corner, then a third time down the next block. Some algorithm deep in my brain tells me he's the same shape as the photographer from the zoo. Now here he is again, half a city away. A tall, slender man with the face of a horse.

—

By the time Mr. Ed finishes dialing his phone in front of the Karachi Press Club, I'm looking for cover. Most explosive devices are detonated by mobile phone, and we're standing at the site of a potential al Qa'ida attack. Is it possible that Jakab got the wrong evening? Possible that I've walked into a trap? It's not worth waiting in the open to find out, especially the day after a fellow operative got nailed across the border.

There's a concrete traffic barrier a few feet to my left. The Pakistani authorities use these as much to stop vehicle-borne explosive devices from reaching sensitive areas as to channel ordinary traffic. It's as good a blast wall as I'm likely to find. I get ready to lunge for it and then stop short. My pocket is vibrating.

I reach for my phone, hit the green button, and press the receiver to my ear.

"Welcome to Karachi," a voice says, and I can see his lips moving across the square. His accent is the distinctive old-world British of the Indian subcontinent. "I wonder if you might have time this evening to pull our meeting forward." He's doing to me what I did to Jakab in Lyon. Shifting control of the meeting logistics to ensure that he has the upper hand. Touché, Mr. Ed. Advantage yours.

After a quick inventory of security considerations, it occurs to me that this might work well. I've already established that I'm not covered by anyone other than the man himself, so no need for tomorrow's SDR. In fact, another night in-country could only serve to raise my profile. That and allowing al Qa'ida to feel that they have a strategic advantage will ensure that they'll be as comfortable and relaxed as possible when I broach a discussion of the attack.

The downside is that HQS won't be spotting me, watching the lines for any sign of trouble the way they would tomorrow. For all I know, the whole thing will be over by then. But if I run into problems in the meantime, no one will even think to check.

Is this how Danny felt, when he walked out of that restaurant and got into a stranger's car? He'd always said that writing the truth meant taking risks. I can only believe he was right. Can only make the same choice, in the name of dialogue, to trust and to go.

"As it happens, that would suit me just fine," I say, and he gives me a slight hint of a bow from afar as he hangs up the phone. I notice, as I walk toward him, that he's wearing red-and-green sandals. It's the first of two predetermined signals telling me I've found the correct person. The second is supposed to be a Coca-Cola in his left hand. He takes a bottle from his bag and holds it up in a mock toast. There's a hint of cockiness to the gesture, a demonstration that he can play by my rules while still insisting that I play by theirs.

Now that I've made the decision to go, I

figure it's best to stay on script, to operate exactly as I would tomorrow. I offer my oral bona fides, a phrase the right person will recognize and respond to in a way that confirms his identity: "Excuse me, do you know where I could find the art museum?"

It's a silly formality, given that he just called my phone. Not much chance he's the wrong guy. But it puts us back on track, and he plays along.

"The art museum is closed today," he replies. "But I could show you to the theater." I nod, then follow him through a maze of back alleyways, mapping the route in my mind as we go, in case I need to make an emergency exit. We pass a street child sitting on a dirty blanket, hand outstretched. Mr. Ed hands the kid the Coke, then turns down another alley before stopping outside a door.

The meeting is with representatives of three extremist groups, all affiliated with al Qa'ida or the Taliban and operating from Karachi to the North-West Frontier Province. The go-between we've used has told them that I have "special channels to Washington." He's told us that they have "access to" al Qa'ida's senior leadership. They've approached us to propose bargains in the past, I've been informed, to limit drone attacks in their territories. HQS has circled them with caution, establishing their credibility and keeping them talking. Today, I need to cut through the circle and get them to talk specifics.

The attack would kill more Muslims than Americans, and I know these three believe that such an action is **haram,** forbidden under Islamic law. After yesterday's bombing, I'm not really in the mood for a theological debate. But we need their help. Convincing them to forbid this bombing is our only available option.

I keep thinking about how this is the same city where Danny was kidnapped, how the people behind his disappearance were one or two connections away from the men I'm about to see. How a colleague died yesterday at the hands of others, not too distant from this group. I'm alone, deep in the belly of the beast, and as we climb each stair to the floor above, the fear pools in the curve of my shoulders and I lock my emotional armor down tight.

We stop at a dusty wooden door, its brown paint chipped to show jagged patches of an earlier green. The man I've been following knocks and calls out the word for "mother." It's an honorific, used to address an older woman with respect. A figure emerges into the hallway, covered with an indigo burqa faded almost to gray. I can make out only the shadow of her brow as I greet her, palm to heart. She asks for my phone, then frisks me, searches my bag, and scans me with a device that can detect radio wave transmissions, to be sure I'm not wired. It's pretty standard choreography. We move through it with respectful caution. She stands still for a minute. I think she is searching my eyes, but I don't know because I can't see hers. Then she says simply "Ii," the word for "yes" in Iraqi Arabic, and the man opens the door into a cramped apartment. The first thing I notice is that the walls are lined with books. The second thing I notice is a baby. And the third thing I notice is that the man holding the baby, bearded and glowering, is the leader of the three men I am there to meet. A feared and battle-hardened jihadi. No intelligence or prep material, nothing in his previous approaches to the Agency has ever suggested anything about his being a dad.

"How old?" I ask.

"Four months," he says, with something that might be tenderness.

"Yours?"

A slight nod.

The baby coughs. A harsh, wet wheeze. There are two other men in the room, both of whom I've met before. I nod wary greetings to each. The courier and the woman have disappeared behind a curtain hung in the hallway doorframe. An M4 leans against the window. The air smells of dust.

I take a seat and begin working my way through the series of questions every operative ticks off at the start of every meeting.

"Are there any urgent security threats I should know about right now?"

"Yes."

An involuntary squirt of adrenaline fans out across my chest.

"Okay, what can you tell me about it?" I ask.

"There are drones in the sky that are killing us like a video game."

I fight the urge to exhale my relief. We both know I meant a threat from somebody other than us. We both know I don't want to make that correction out loud. There's nothing for it but to meet it head-on.

"Other than the threats you face from the United States and coalition forces"—I pause and we exchange a look of mutual acknowledgment—"are there any urgent threats I should know about before we get started."

He shakes his head slowly. The baby wheezes again.

"How much time do we have?"

He gives a slight side nod, meaning "As much as I want to give you."

The woman reappears with a tray holding a teapot, glass cups in metal filigree holders, and sugar cubes in a bowl.

I describe the threat reporting I'm there about.

"Most of the dead will be your brothers and sisters in Islam." I reach for the tourist map in my bag, moving slowly to keep everyone at ease. Roll it out on the table, using my teacup as a weight. "There are vehicle barriers here and here, meaning the truck will probably detonate here, the closest it can get to the press club or the bank. This building here is a community center. This is a mosque. This and this are both schools. This is a health clinic."

"And this"—he cuts me off, his finger tapping the location of the small wooden shed alongside the press club's gates—"is a flower shop." He smiles at me. A sad, resigned smile. "I know the area well. Why are you coming to me with this?"

"Because I know you are a man of honor. And a man of God. You don't believe it's acceptable in God's sight to kill innocents or followers of Islam."

"This is true. But if I object to this attack

based on the risk to Muslims, they will choose an alternative target. One where the dead will be exclusively Americans. Would you prefer this?"

"No," I answer. "I would prefer them not to attack any target at all."

"And you will abide by this, too?"

"How do you mean," I ask.

"You will also not attack any target at all?" The baby wheezes.

"Only legitimate targets," I say.

"What are those?" he asks.

"Areas used to stage bombings."

"So we may attack the areas where you stage bombings."

"No, we may. You may not."

There is a pause. Just traffic and the baby's sticky breath.

"Why?"

"You and I both know you can't get close to the places where we stage our strikes. To get to them means killing civilians as well."

In my head I add, "Like you did yesterday, asshole, when you blew up a slew of Afghans along with one of my friends."

"Such is also the case with your drones," he replies. "Just ask my wife." It's unclear whether he means that his wife is dead or that someone she loves is dead.

"There is too much tolerance for civilian casualties on both sides," I concede.

"The difference," he says, "is we tolerate killing civilians to get you out of our country. And you tolerate killing civilians to stay here."

There is a pause. I can sense his wife and my friends and the thousands of tit-for-tat dead, there with us in the dust. I look at the baby, her little chest working to pull oxygen through the filter of mucus I can hear in her throat. I feel Zoë inside me.

"Asthma?" I ask. He nods. "I have a little one, too," I tell him. "We live in China." His posture shifts. He gives me a look of knowing sympathy, parent to parent, lamenting governments' inability to keep the air clean. "She has trouble breathing sometimes too. Have you ever tried clove oil?" I ask. He shakes his head.

Clove oil has always worked when Zoë begins to cough. I happen to have some in my backpack. I take a vial along when I'm operational because it's helpful in making certain inks, if I need to adjust alias documents on the go. And it's an antibacterial and bug repellent, so it doesn't look suspicious.

I pull out the dark glass bottle, like a Shakespearean apothecary, and offer it to him.

"You need to dilute it, because it's very strong. Put some in hot water and let the baby inhale the steam." I hold it in the air, but he doesn't move to take it. I realize the extent of the leap I'm asking him to make. To trust me, a representative of the country that's trying to kill him. To let his child inhale the unidentified contents of my bottle, on the off chance that I'm sincere. I take the top off and breathe in, to demonstrate the oil's safety. Then close it up again and set the vial on the table.

He squints at me, like he's trying to make something out. The room feels like that old optical illusion, the one that can be seen as a vase or else two faces in profile. As operatives, he and I are on different sides of this struggle, fighting each other. As parents, we're on the same side, fighting for our kids' right to breathe. We both sense a choice, in that clove-drenched moment: whether to focus on the two opposing faces or the single unified vase.

The woman reappears briefly and places a branch of small white flowers on the table. Something in her movement suggests that she might be his mother. And also the boss.

"Alyssum," he says, working the snowy blossoms off the branch and into a tidy pile atop the tourist map. "Tastes like broccoli." He smiles and pops a flower into his mouth, a reciprocal gesture of reassurance.

"For asthma?" I ask. He nods.

"Trade you." I pick up one of the flowers and he takes a sniff of the clove vial, both of us cautious, our noses wrinkled like children trying new food. Slowly, we both start laughing. The other two men in the room do not.

"Look," I say. "You're right. They'll pick new targets. We'll all pick new targets. We can't save everyone. But we can save the young woman who may be standing at that flower stall. We can save the kids playing in that schoolyard, same as yours and mine will be. The Qur'an says that to save one innocent life is to save all humankind. Could we try and save humankind today? Even if it destroys itself again tomorrow?"

There's a long pause. Then he offers an almost imperceptible nod. The other two fighters break into rapid-fire Urdu. One reaches for the weapon against the wall; the other takes a hard step toward me. I fight the urge to run. Instead, I hold their leader's eye and put my hand to my heart to convey respect. He raises his fingers slightly from the tabletop, and the other men stop short. I fold the map around the white flowers, slide the tube into my backpack, every muscle in my body aware of the M4 now cradled in the arms of the fighter farthest from me. To show any suspicion that he might fire it would be to suggest that he would disrespect his leader—an insult to both of them, and a sure way to end up in a jumpsuit. Instead, I take my time zipping up my pack and pause to finish my tea. In my peripheral vision, I feel the fighter's posture relax. The leader's eyes crinkle slightly, as if in response to a private joke.

"The alyssum is also good for stress," he says. I smile as I get up to leave.

"And the clove oil will help with teething." It's an intentional choice we both make to end the meeting as parents, not as operatives. An unspoken agreement to interpret our picture as one vase today, instead of two opposing faces.

On my way out the door, my fingers brush the chipped brown paint and the green showing through underneath. I think of my grandmother, peeling back the dead exterior of the rose stems in her garden to find the white-green rawness of fresh life inside. I think of the parks in Hanoi and Berlin and Tokyo where air strikes once rained fire. And I remember the little sign in my neighbor's front yard when I was a kid. It said, "Planting a garden is the ultimate act of faith in tomorrow."

—

It's not until I'm back in Shanghai, listening to **Peter and the Wolf** with Zoë, that I find out whether those particular seeds took root. I receive a follow-up cable on the day of the intended attack. UNEVENTFUL AFTERNOON. APPEARS THREAT DEFERRED OR NEW TARGET ACQUIRED. KUDOS. I think of the dusty room and the wheezing baby, with her nostrils flared wide. I think of her dad, making choices to protect her—from pollution and air strikes and drones. I think about how everybody believes that they are the good guy. And how the trick of the thing is seeing that, from one angle or another, we all actually are.

"Well, that's a hundred or so fewer families that'll grow up hating you," I say to Zoë as I take her into the kitchen to get dinner started.

19

In 2009, when I'm twenty-eight and Zoë is not yet quite one, we return to Washington so that Dean can undergo an advanced surveillance detection course, the same one I completed while he was in Afghanistan. I have lunch with my old boss Jon in the HQS courtyard beside a giant metal sculpture covered in encrypted code. He tells me about an argument his team is having with a Middle Eastern government. "They're offering us all this shit we don't need. But they won't do the one thing we do need until we give them something else," he says.

"So why don't you give it to them?" I ask.

"'Cause we don't have it, smart-ass! But we're not gonna fuckin' tell them that. They think our coverage out there is way better than it is. If they knew we were this weak, they'd crush us. Or just fucking ignore us."

I laugh. "So you're pissed they're not offering you the one thing you need even though you've told them you already have it."

He punches me in the arm. "You sound like my marriage counselor."

Later, he texts me to meet him for a drink. "Swami G!" he calls out when I arrive. "Took your advice and told them what we wanted."

I laugh because I can tell from his cranky gratitude that it turned out okay. "And . . . ?"

He drops a shot into his Guinness, takes a swig, and says, "And they gave it to us."

I signal the bartender for a drink and give Jon a smile that says, "Imagine that!"

He laughs, but there's a sadness in it. "Too bad we weren't channeling all this 'Confucius say' shit before the whole goddamned thing got started. Could have saved Tim some work."

Tim's the guy who carves stars on the wall.

I walk home and find Dean asleep in prep for early morning surveillance training. Zoë is sleeping soundly on the blanket Dean brought back from Afghanistan. I walk past all the surveillance maps spread across the desk and the floor. Trace the intricate patterns of skillful paranoia marked with the instructor's pen. Tidy the hats and wigs and shirts piled by the door to alternate as light disguises. Turn the extra dead bolt. And stand for a minute on the inside of this fortress of professional pretend, feeling less safe than I had outside the door.

When I hear Zoë stir, I wrap her up in the Afghan blanket, unlock the locks, and take her back out under the stars. "There is the String of Pearls," I tell her, as she falls back to sleep. And in the cricket-filled night, I smile to Mahmoud, half a world away. Hear his words, from years ago: "We're not so different as we pretend to be, you know."

—

After the murk-filled skies of Shanghai, the Virginia mornings taste clean. The American flags that flutter from buildings on my way to Langley remind me this country is still in motion; it's a work in progress, this experiment in government of and by and for the people. We don't always get it right. But after living under a government that censors the Internet and imprisons families for going to church, I swell with gratitude that we keep striving, drawing ever closer in our asymptote to freedom.

My brother Ben comes to visit, and we walk

and talk in the same streets we used to roam as children. He's found his calling providing end-of-life care at a hospice, holding vigil at the bedsides of the dying in their final days of life.

"What do you say to them?" I ask him.

"I tell them to think of me as a big wooden chest they can put all their stories in," he says. "So they know their stories will be preserved when they are gone." After the teasing of his youth, his tenderness makes me marvel.

"Thank you for being my big brother," I say, as we pass the patches of mulberry leaves we used to pick to feed his silkworms.

My sisters are growing into dynamos of community care all their own. Both are still in school—Antonia to become an early childhood educator, and Catherine a peer counselor. I am in awe of my dazzling mother, who painted our world with color and inspired each of us to, in our own way, make our communities heathier, happier, safer, smarter.

Even my father visits from time to time, full of tales about his adventures building out the developing world's electrical grids, ensuring light where once there was none. It's taken a long time to see him as my dad again, after he left our mom so injured and us kids to pick up the pieces. But time has passed and the grayscale of adulthood has replaced the black-and-white judgments of my youth. Mom is happier now, and in seeing her laugh again, I begin to forgive my dad, begin to let myself love him fully for the first time in years.

It's cathartic, to be back among family, makes me aware of how much I've changed since I first applied to the Agency in that post-9/11 haze of oversimplification and fear. I begin to metabolize the lessons I've learned in the field, realize more fully that peacemaking requires listening, that vulnerability is a component of strength. I think of Emmett's kung fu and the sticker in the Karachi taxi-cab. "Remember, the other person is you."

As operations ramp back up, Dean senses the shift in me, bristles at my quiet mention that a situation might be more complicated than it seems. Drone killings and enhanced interrogation become subjects of dread on the operations we plan in tandem. Each time I opt for a different choice, he takes it personally, a critique of his tradecraft, a rebuttal to his way of life, an abandonment of him. I find that building trust simply works better than exerting force. Detention simply works better than assassination. They are pragmatic decisions, the fastest, cheapest, most reliable way to save lives and prevent attacks. But Dean hears them as a condemnation of the moonless nights he spent in Afghanistan, firing at moving shapes to prevent them from firing at him. He takes it as judgment, for inflicting pain, for fighting death with death.

He begins to feel he's lost his only ally, the girl who wrote him love letters when he was deployed to a world of fear. It makes him anger easily, makes him hit things— first dashboards and tables, then cupboards and walls. Never Zoë and never me. But the angrier he gets, the more things he breaks. One day he puts his fist through plaster, then disappears, then returns crying, apologizing, curls up on the floor, in the fetal position and in pain. I lie behind him, fit my body to his like a spoon, reliving the past together on the cold, hard ground. I desperately want to make it better. But it feels like the only thing I can say is nothing at all. We reacquaint ourselves with silence. Talk only to our baby girl. And in both our cases, I think, though separately, to God.

One day I make us tea in mugs my mother bought us from a camping store. Big and comfy and rustic, with country glazing. One says "Love" and the other "Peace." But the letters are subtle, the same color as the mugs themselves, and I don't notice that I've given Dean the mug that says "Peace" until he throws it at the wall. The cup smashes. The tea splatters, then drips down to the floor. He picks Zoë up from her high chair, looks into her face, and says, "Your mother's a cunt, you know that?"

She's too young to understand the word. And I'm too old not to hear the pain behind it. I shouldn't have given him that mug, should have realized it might come across as criticism of all that he's sacrificed, all that he's done. In that moment, we understand that we don't know how to fix each other. I hold my arms out to him, silently asking for our daughter. He gives her to me, already apologizing with his eyes. I'm crying. So is he. We hold each other's gaze for a minute, allowing ourselves to be seen.

Then he gives me a nod. And I leave.

—

When Dean next deploys, I don't go with him. It takes time to dissolve an Agency marriage, but it feels final as soon as his plane pulls away from the private air terminal; he's on his way back to the mountains of Afghanistan, returning to the fight on behalf of his country and his principles and our daughter. I think of all that's happened since we first met in that gazebo at the Farm. Day by day, the responsibility of lives in our hands has aged us, the trauma of knowing the wrong choice may mean death—our own or someone else's. I wonder what our relationship might have been in the normal world, without the sacrifices that first drew us closer and then tugged us apart. We haven't always agreed on the best way to end this war, but we've given dearly, given separately and together, to make the killing stop.

I sit in the front seat of my old Jeep and watch from the end of the runway, Zoë asleep on my shoulder, as the metal tube containing her dad takes to the air. In that moment, I know he would do anything to protect us, know how lucky our daughter is to have the father that she does. I watch as the plane grows smaller, watch until it disappears completely and the sky is still. We're alone except for a bird, moving about in the tree beside the car. I have the same feeling I had beside the lake after the siren sounded at the end of our time at the Farm—the feeling of glimpsing a theater's bare stage between one play and the next. The stage is unalterable. But what we players do on it—our story lines, our conflicts, our drama—"Well, that's on us, huh?" I ask my sleeping daughter as I fasten her into the car seat to head for home.

I get asked to deploy again, this time in alias—false identities for both Zoë and me. "She's young enough not to remember," the Agency shrink assures me. And I know that he's right. But something in me bucks at the request. I finger the necklace I'm wearing—a bronze letter Z, for Zoë, for life. I imagine packing it away, along with our true selves, and teaching my child to respond to a different name. I listen to the briefings, assess the approach. It's all pretty secure. They're right. We can win this one by outdeceiving the other side. But I can't shake the feeling that it won't end there. As we stand in that room, huddled around a whiteboard, it feels like an endless hall of mirrors, with all the past deception that got us here behind us and all the future deceptions this operation will make necessary unfolding ahead. An infinite sequence of whiteboards, covered in well-intentioned lies.

"I'm gonna go hit the head," I tell them.

On the way back, Jon stops me in the hall.

"Doesn't look to me like you're too into this one," he says.

"Yeah, well, guess that's the service part of service," I laugh.

"Nope," he says, "the service part of service is doing the thing you're called to do."

I look down. I know he's thinking I've gone soft since I had my girl. And he's right. But what he doesn't understand yet is that soft works. Soft is how we end this war. The Agency taught me to fight terrorism by convincing my enemy that I'm scary. Zoë taught me to fight by taking off my mask and showing my enemy that I'm human. In that hallway, surrounded by metal vault doors that lead into giant airtight rooms of secrets, I know that both paths might lead to security, but only Zoë's path leads to actual peace.

"Look, you've given us almost a decade," he says. "You've racked up awards and blah blah. Helped save a bunch of lives. I sure as shit don't want to lose you. But this place is like a swimming pool. No matter how much space you take up while you're in it, the water'll close around you when you get out and no one will ever know you're missing." I look at him for a minute and he adds, "That's a crotchety old man's way of saying, 'You did good, kid. Your country's in your debt. It's okay to do what's next.'"

I walk outside and sit next to the Berlin Wall panels as the sun falls behind the woods. This has been my world since I was twenty-two years old. My one underlying truth as battles and relationships have come and gone. But in my heart I know that Langley and I have given each other all we're supposed to. I don't address Him directly, but it's God I'm talking to when I whisper out loud, "Use me. Please use me. Show me my next work."

That night, Zoë drops a book in my lap. It's **The Velveteen Rabbit**. I read it to her as my eyes well with tears: "You become. It takes a long time. That's why it doesn't happen often to people who break easily, or have sharp edges, or who have to be carefully kept. Generally, by the time you are Real, most of your hair has been loved off, and your eyes drop out and you get loose in the joints and very shabby. But these things don't matter at all, because once you are Real you can't be ugly, except to people who don't understand."

I'm not sure yet what my work in the world will be, but I know that I need to do it without any disguises to hide behind. I submit my letter of resignation and make my way through a wistful week of lasts—last contribution to the President's Daily Brief, last pitcher of beer with my brothers-in-arms, last time through the badge machine and out the eastern doors, with the cicadas singing an undulating good-bye in the thick summer wet. I drive out the gates to Route 123, past the snipers and over the tire hazards, aware that there's no returning now, except through the visitors' entrance. I turn left, drop down onto Rock Creek Parkway, and head for home.

There's traffic on Key Bridge, the Lincoln Memorial to my right and the Georgetown boathouse to my left. In the quiet of my car, I examine myself in the mirror. Touch my cheek. I've worn masks for almost a decade. My real face feels inchoate and raw, like the moist paleness of new skin beneath a Band-Aid. The light at the end of the bridge turns green and the traffic begins to move. Zoë's waiting for me. I shift into gear and roll slowly forward.

20

We move to California to be near my mom and stepdad, who are renovating an old house in the foothills of Santa Barbara. Tucked into a nearby wooden cottage, not far from the sea, I begin the process of peeling off my fictions like layer after layer of onion. I put down the fearlessness and the coolness and the strength. Learn to say "I don't know." I discover that becoming Real isn't as simple as driving out through the Langley gates. It isn't only undercover spies who pretend. It's everyone with a social media account, it turns out, or a lover or a boss. At first it confuses me, why these people would lie without the same stakes on the line. I get angry, because I'm disappointed in them, but more because I'm disappointed in myself, in how I'm no more Real in California than I was in Shanghai.

One day, my mom writes me a letter, and I read it next to the crashing Pacific Ocean. She can see that I'm struggling, can empathize with my journey to find and inhabit my true self. People pretend in the real world just as much as in the spy world, she says. They pretend because the stakes are the same—the stakes are not getting hurt. Sure, in my old world the harm was a suitcase nuke in Times Square, but who's to say the scorn of a lover isn't as powerful a weapon? Problem is, she points out, the cost of the armor is the same, too. The insecurity that comes from building relationships on a lie, on a flickering projection of strength.

I think of my old boss and his Mideast negotiations—remember asking him how our allies can give us something we won't tell them we lack. Turns out, the same goes for friends. And spouses. And moms.

Whether it's falling in love or starting a movement, talking with a coworker or building up NATO, pretending makes us feel strong, she says, in relationships and geopolitics. It makes us feel safe. But pretending is a shoddy foundation for things like peace and power. She tells me how she's grown from an unsure young mother, afraid of not looking or speaking or acting as she should.

How honest vulnerability, paradoxically, has made her strong. How that strength, that Realness, has sustained her friendships and second marriage in a way the pretending of youth never could. I watch the waves crash against the seawall and thank the universe for gifting me my mother, my rock, my guiding point of light. I feel the power of opening ourselves up, with no pretense at armor. Not just in Karachi and Fallujah and Aleppo, but here at home as well.

Slowly, I begin getting involved in my local community—in corrections facilities and homeless shelters—working with gang members to build trust using the same skills I honed on the streets of the Middle East. I write to my old boss Jon to tell him I've found the work I left the Agency to do—the work to which Zoë and my mother led me: ending conflict through vulnerable, honest human exchange. I work with violent offenders, preparing them to meet their victims. I travel back to Iraq and Jordan and Turkey, taking Sunni and Shi'ite militia members through the same program of reconciliation in the ever-growing settlements of refugees. Sitting beside resting weapons, I watch as men accustomed to firing at one another share tea and tears instead. Every time I witness one of these honest moments between enemies, it feels like the lifting of a spell, the victims of a fairy tale curse slowly waking, blinking in the light, as they recognize one another as human. I watch their first agreements take hold in the camps they govern. Watch their children walk to school together in safety.

"Think this old dog could learn those new tricks?" Jon asks me on the phone one day.

"Thought you'd never ask!" I laugh. Retired from Langley, he's at my side on my next trip to Iraq, the two of us sitting on the floor, cross-legged, in circles of Sunni and Shi'ite teenagers who've lost family members to one another's parents. Not so long ago, we were fighting on this very soil. Today, the air is thick with hurt and healing. At the afternoon's end, Jon tells me about the moment he knew it was going to be okay. "When that girl sat there and held hands with the kid of the guy who killed her brother and said, 'We have to honor our parents by not repeating their mistakes.'" He makes a gesture like his heart just exploded.

"Let's hope our kids honor us the same way, huh?" I laugh and we walk the long, dusty path to the refugee camp gates, old brother- and sister-in-arms, reassured at having glimpsed a future that is better than we are.

—

Back home, I begin to build a life, and a family of friends who know my truth. Zoë and I make dinners in the kitchen of our little wooden cottage and eat them on the roof looking up at the stars, then fall asleep in my big quilt-covered bed, with the ocean ever-constant and ever-changing outside our door. There is a hugeness in this small life—a flame that reveals itself in the stillness. And the more I feel it, the more scared I am that it will get invaded by the chaotic world beyond.

When I'm invited to speak publicly about my work, my body physically revolts, like jerking my fingers back from a hot stove.

"I get it," the journalist jokes. "You want to keep all your lessons locked up so only you can enjoy them."

"No," I laugh, "I'm just scared of—" I pause.

"Of . . ." he prompts me.

Every instinct and every piece of training I've ever undergone is in opposition to this moment. What will happen if I tell the world the truth? Spill that most secret of secrets: that all we soldiers and spies, all the belching, booming armored juggernauts of war, all the terror groups and all the rogue states, that we're all just pretending to be fierce because we're all on fire with fear. What will happen if I speak those words out loud? Will I get hurt? Will Zoë get hurt? Will our life be disrupted all over again? But then I remember my daughter, looking up at me and laughing. I think of the white flowers on the table in Karachi and the girls sitting in their dusty circle outside Mosul. Of the prisoners, here at home, making amends to their victims and themselves. Of the gang members removing their tattoos. I think of my brother, holding the hands of the dying.

"Of nothing," I answer.

And instead of hiding, I sit in front of a camera and tell the world the truth.

It's indescribable. After a lifetime of social expectations and war games and strategy. Indescribably liberating to speak with no filter of fear. And not just for me, it turns out. My words spread fast. Millions, then tens of millions, then a hundred million people watch. Soon I start receiving e-mails from veterans around the world—Americans and Afghans and Russians and Egyptians. Each of them like the Wizard of Oz, trapped behind their curtains, shouting at one another with ever-bigger voices. And each of them finally brave enough, in those halting, nervous e-mails, to let the curtain drop—to show themselves as human and be free.

I read the new messages each morning, introduce the writers to one another, letter by vulnerable letter, a slowly growing web of peace. And as I read, I glance, every so often, at the coin that still sits on my desk, finger the engraving, worn down like a compass that is battered but truer with use. I think about how much more deeply I understand its words now than when I first read them, flushed with excitement as a CIA trainee.

"And ye shall know the truth and the truth shall make you free."

Acknowledgments

To the women and men of CIA, your work is hard and mostly unrecognized. You grapple with questions of ethics and law, life and death. You do not have the luxury of armchair quarterbacking or passing the buck. You work in the shadow of potential apocalypse, costing human lives and dreams. Your allegiance is to the flag, to the Constitution, to some higher power, be that God or Love. I came of age in your midst. I marinated in the tradition of service you modeled for me. Thank you for making me the woman I've become.

Lisa, you mean it when you tell people you love them. You bring them soup when they're sick. You keep their secrets. You have their back. I nearly don't remember life without you. I learned friendship at your side. Thank you for making me the woman I've become.

Acknowledgments

Min Zin and Daryl, you work for democracy at ongoing cost to your comfort and safety. You tell the truth when the world is not ready or is not interested. You stand by those who suffer for freedom and live the words you speak. In your shadows, I learned the power of individual citizens to change the world. Thank you for making me the woman I've become.

Emmett, you see the worth in people, whether or not they see it in themselves. You commit your hours to the uplifting of others. You see the world for what it could be and do more than your part to manifest the evolution. Across continents and email addresses, I learned from what you wrote me and I learned from what I wrote you. I found in you proof that humans could be both cool and good. And I witnessed the dividends introspection can pay. I admire the man you are. Thank you for making me the woman I've become.

Anthony, you devote your brain and being to the expression of truth through art. You are kind and loyal. You are clever without being small. You were the first person I fell in love with and the first person I properly hurt. You taught me to recognize how far I have yet to go. And the responsibility I bear for getting there without harming others as I grow. I've held your wisdom close these last two decades. Thank you for making me the woman I've become.

Jon, you are a national treasure, though most people walk past you on the street unaware. You have spent decades in service of a country that cannot thank you because they do not know your name. You are the most skilled operator I know. And a gracious teacher. You gave me the space I needed to fail and the tools I needed to succeed. Deep bow to you, my mentor and friend. Thank you for making me the woman I've become.

Dean, you are a patriot. You are a friend. You are an incredible dad. The world is safer because of your work in the field and our daughter is the young woman she is because of your love at home. We've walked a wild journey together. At your side, I learned to talk less and listen more. I learned to put mission before comfort. I learned the many faces love can have. Thank you for making me the woman I've become.

Meg, Dr. Platt, Father Davies, you live between the spiritual and terrestrial realms. You are on conversational terms with God. You have walked beside me in my faith journey. You have asked and answered questions of purpose and courage. You have uncovered

Acknowledgments

for me the suchness of life. You have shown me why I am here. Thank you for making me the woman I've become.

Jordan, Erin, Anna, Michael, Lynette, Brie, you shape tomorrow's reality through the telling of stories, the sharing of human experience. You amplify voices of hope. You give people reason to believe. I cannot imagine a more capable or inspiring team. I get to share this story because of you. Thank you for making me the woman I've become.

James, Dani, Clare, Kate, and Chris, you taught me the meaning of unconditional love. You nurtured and forgave me without asking anything in return. You taught me how to be vulnerable. You taught me how to be happy. You taught me how to be. Thank you for making me the woman I've become.

Mum, Steven, Dad, Luda, Ben, Eva, Antonia, Sasha, Catherine, you are my homeland, my country of origin. You know me as no one else can. In your protective circle, I learned who I was. You loved me, even when I didn't deserve it. Especially when I didn't deserve it. I bear our family flag across my heart. Thank you for making me the woman I've become.

Zoë and Bobcat, you are my teachers. You are funny and brave. You are kind. You carry inside you the echoes of my mother. You are proof of immortality. I cannot wait to see the paths you will walk. My paw is forever in yours. Thank you for making me the woman I've become.

Bobby, you are a man who has seen the deep truth of the universe and you live that truth each day. You prize family, friends, and art above belongings and material wealth. You lead with humility. You excel quietly. You give without expectation of recognition. You are the person who most inspires me. My electric collaborator, my place of rest. You would recognize my soul outside my spaceship. I have let your spirit inside its walls. My partner in creativity and creation, thank you for making my heart whole.

A Note About the Author

Following her CIA career in the field, Amaryllis Fox has covered current events and offered analysis for CNN, the National Geographic channel, Al Jazeera, the BBC, and other global news outlets. She speaks at events and universities around the world on the topic of peacemaking. She is the host of the upcoming Netflix series **The Business of Drugs** and lives in Los Angeles with her husband and daughters.